ABOUT THE AUTHOR

Jessica Bell is an award-winning author/poet, writing/ publishing coach, graphic designer, and singer-songwriter who was born in Melbourne, Australia. She currently resides in Athens, Greece.

In addition to having published a memoir, four novels, three poetry collections, and her bestselling Writing in a Nutshell series, she has been featured in a variety of publications and ABC Radio National shows such as *Writer's Digest*, *Publisher's Weekly*, *The Guardian*, *Life Matters*, and *Poetica*.

She is also the Publisher of Vine Leaves Press, CEO of Independent Publishing Assistance, a voice-over actor, and the coordinator of the Writing Day Workshops.

In October 2016, she became the new lead singer of the well-known dream-pop group, Keep Shelly In Athens, and records and performs as a solo artist under the name BRUNO.

Visit: *iamjessicabell.com*

self PUBLISH YOUR BOOK

A QUICK & EASY STEP-BY-STEP GUIDE

Jessica Bell

Vine Leaves Press
Melbourne, Vic, Australia

CONTENTS

To all writers out there who need something to be easy for once.

i

INTRODUCTION

G'day! It's Jessica again with another Nutshell book. If you're new to the "Writing in a Nutshell" series, welcome! Hopefully this book will make your life a little easier, and save you precious time and money. Before I get down to business, I'd like first to establish whether this book is for you.

This book is for you if your book is ready for publication and you can answer "true" to one or more of the following statements:

- *I have never self-published before and have no idea what I'm doing.*
- *I have never self-published before, don't want to spend any money doing so, but still want to end up with a quality product.*
- *I have never self-published before and I'm looking for the quickest, most hassle-free, and cheapest way to do so.*

- *I have only self-published with a vanity publisher before and am not happy with their service.*
- *I have self-published before, but I have always hired freelancers to do all the work and need some guidance to take control and save money.*
- *I have self-published before, but I am not happy with the quality of my work and need some help to make it better this time.*
- *I have self-published before, but it took me so long, and cost me so much money—I need help getting organized to help manage my time.*

Now, you may also be wondering, why another book on self-publishing? Isn't the market saturated with these types of books already? And what can I tell you that another book can't? Well, you may have a point, but the beauty of my Nutshell books is that they do not overwhelm you with all the information available—they tell you specifically what you need to know, without all the faff, and follow one particular method.

If you're the type of person, like me, who needs to tick things off a list to feel organized, then you're reading the right book. This self-publishing guide offers you a step-by-step, foolproof, cost-efficient, time-efficient, extremely easy-to-follow process for making your books available for sale. Sometimes I may cut in very briefly with an alternative to what I'm proposing, but I promise the interruption will be short and to the point, and most likely lead you to another resource in case you'd like to know more.

You'll notice that there are black and white picture aids at the back of the book which will help you to better understand my instructions. Whenever a picture aid is necessary, I will tell you to refer to it. If you would like to see these pictures in colour (and much bigger!), you can download the PDF file from ***howtoselfpublishyourbook.net/templates.html***. You will be prompted to enter this password to gain access: selfpub101.

So ... are you ready to get started?

ii

COMPUTER
SOFTWARE NEEDED

DIY Self-Publishing cannot be DIY if you don't have specific software to help you out. If you don't already have the following software, I suggest you get it, especially if you intend to self-publish more books completely on your own.

You are going to need the following software to fulfil every step in this book:

1. Microsoft Word (free for a 30-day trial) to prepare your manuscript and paperback interior layout;
2. Adobe Photoshop (free for a 30-day trial) to design your cover;
3. Adobe Acrobat Pro DC (free for a 30-day trial), which is a PDF creator and editor for your printable cover and interior;
4. Notepad++ (free for life) to format your eBook; and

5. Calibre (free for life) to convert your eBook into a retail-ready file.

In addition to the above, I use InDesign to do the paperback interior layout, but you can also format paperbacks efficiently and professionally in Microsoft Word (which is what I used to do in the beginning), so for the sake of making your life easier, I'm not going to refer to InDesign at all in this book. Also, please note that I am a PC user, so any computer commands will refer to those on a PC. For Mac commands, a simple Internet search will help you out if you don't already know the equivalents.

Let me tell you a few things about the software above and why I've chosen these programs for you. They are compatible with all computers and the other software, so I strongly suggest you do not skimp on alternative programs like Open Office, or use Pages (for Mac), for example. You could end up with extraordinarily frustrating technical problems down the line. I won't go into details, so you're just going to have to trust me on that. I've been doing this for a long time and have heard many horror stories about formatting that would have been avoided had the authors been using standard software.

A small word of caution: not every person is going to own the same version of the software used in this book. If you already own the software I recommend, you may have older versions than I do. If you don't already own the software, you are going to end up with newer versions than I have. Because this book is extremely specific with its instructions, you are bound to come across a few steps that do not match 100% to what you see on your computer at home. This is unavoidable and I urge you not to fret. If something looks different to how I show it, and you can't seem to find something, simply click F1 on your keyboard for *Help*. And you also have Google. I learnt everything I know about self-publishing from the Internet and through a lot of trial and error. If you have a question, the answer is most definitely somewhere in cyberspace.

1

PREPARE YOUR MANUSCRIPT IN MICROSOFT WORD

You may think your manuscript is fine until you start commanding Word to do specific tasks and strange things begin happening. For example, if you have used tabs or spaces for the start of your paragraphs, instead of proper indents, you're going to face formatting problems later on. For example, your paragraph indents may not be aligned properly.

Note: This section is not going to tell you how to edit your manuscript. Your book should be edited and ready for publication. For information on self-editing, please refer to my book *Polish Your Fiction: A Quick & Easy Self-Editing Guide*.

MANUSCRIPT PREPARATION STEP-BY-STEP:

1. Make a copy of your manuscript in case you make an irreversible mistake.

2. Show all formatting (Ctrl + Shift + 8). You will now see all the formatting marks, such as paragraph breaks, tabs, and spaces.

3. Firstly, remove any instances of double spaces after full stops. You may have been taught this in school, but it is frowned upon nowadays. To do this:
- Open the *Find and Replace* dialog box (Ctrl + H).
- Type in two spaces in the *Find* field and one space in the *Replace* field.
- Click *Replace All*. (Do this multiple times until the dialogue box says there were 0 replacements.)
- Keep in mind that this might change any formatting where you purposefully used spacing (e.g. poems or song lyrics).

Also, for some reason—and it happens to me too—you end up with an extra useless space at the end of paragraphs. It's a good idea to clean this up. All you have to do is replace *.[space]^p* with *. ^p* and they will disappear.

Note: Do not literally type *[space]*; it means to press the space bar.

4. Find out what you have done at the beginning of new paragraphs. If there are tabs (or spaces) instead of indents:
- Open the *Find and Replace* dialogue box (Ctrl + H).
- Place your cursor in the *Find* field and then click *More* (at the bottom left).

- Now click *Special* and select *Tab Character*.
- Leave the *Replace* field blank and click *Replace All*.

If you've used spaces, just select the *Paragraph Mark* from the *Special* menu and type the amount of spaces you've used after it into the *Find* field. If the amount of space you've used is inconsistent, you'll have to do this a few times.

5. Now all your indents will be gone, but you will fix this now. (Refer to Pic. 1a on page 83 for visual.)
- Open the *Paragraph* group box located in the *Home* tab.
- In the *Indentation* section, select *First line* under *Special*.
- Now under *By*, type in *0.2*. (If your Word is set to centimetres rather than inches, type in *0.6*.)
- Make sure *Left* and *Right* are set to *0*. (While you're in there, make sure in the *Spacing* section your *Before* and *After* are set to *0*, and *Line spacing* is set to *Single*.)
- Now click *OK*.

Your indents are now back and formatted properly.

6. If you have used any automatic numbering or bullet points, disable them and insert your numbers and lists manually. Pain in the butt? Maybe, but it will save you a headache later on as all automatic formatting will disappear when it's time to format your eBook. I won't go into that until later on, so please take my word for it.

To disable your automatic numbering and bulleting:
- Click the *Microsoft Office Button* (top left of your screen) and then click *Word Options* (bottom right of dialog box).
- Click *Proofing*.
- Click *AutoCorrect Options*, and then click the *AutoFormat As You Type* tab.

- Under *Apply as you type*, clear the *Automatic bulleted lists* tick box and/or the *Automatic numbered lists* tick box.

7. If you have used italics at all, please make sure only the word or sentence is italicized. What I mean by that is, the spaces, full stops, and/or paragraph marks before and after the italicized section should be completely free of that formatting. Again this has to do with saving you a headache later when formatting your eBook. The same goes for bolding and underlining.

Tips:
1. 0.2 inches (0.6 cm) is an ideal indent size for both paperback and eBook.
2. It's customary *not* to indent the first line of a new chapter or section. Paragraphs should only be indented if there is another paragraph preceding it. To remove the indent from the very first line of a new chapter or section, go to the start of each chapter or section and place the cursor at the beginning of the first paragraph. Follow the procedure on how to set an indent, but select *None* instead of *First line*. Do the same for your chapter headings and anything that might be centred (e.g. asterisks used for a line break) because they will have been indented as well.
3. Please do not use line spaces to separate paragraphs in fiction. It's common for nonfiction, but in fiction it just wastes space, especially when you have a lot of dialogue together, as each utterance generally starts on a new line.

Note: If you feel you need more guidance for preparing your manuscript please refer to "Section 2.2 Typographical Considerations" in *Polish Your Fiction: A Quick & Easy Self-Editing Guide.*

2

DESIGN YOUR EBOOK COVER

I know what you're thinking: isn't this a little premature? I don't even have the interior of my book done yet—and what about the paperback cover?

Don't stress. You're doing the eBook cover now for a very good reason. You need to know what fonts you are going to use on the cover so that you can use the same fonts inside the book for the title page and your chapter headings. Matching the look of the interior with the cover will leave you with a professional-looking quality product.

I design book covers professionally, and I do all sorts of weird and wonderful tricks which, unfortunately, I'm not going to be able to teach you. To teach you these things would mean giving you a fully-fledged tutorial on how to use

Adobe Photoshop and gifting you with my experience. And regardless, I'm sure that's not what you want out of reading this book. You want quick and easy, right?

So what I'm going to do is offer you tips on how to make a very simple yet striking cover, and give you an easy-to-use Adobe Photoshop template from which you can start and tweak to your heart's content.

Note: I currently use Adobe Photoshop CC, but it will continue to update automatically as I am subscribed to Adobe. If you are also subscribed and read this book when the program has updated to a newer version, I want you to know that this should not cause you any problems when trying to follow my instructions in this book as the program interface does not significantly change. But there will be very slight differences. If you get stuck, press F1 for *Help*.

Before I move on with the step-by-step procedure, I'd like to explain a few things so you can better understand what will make a striking cover regardless of how simple a design it is.

- Firstly, download the eBook Cover Template from *howtoselfpublishyourbook.net/templates.html* (remember to enter this password to gain access: selfpub101) so that I can explain the elements to you while you're looking at it.
- Save the .psd file to your desired location and open it.
- Click *File* and then *Save As*, to save it as your own book cover with a different file name. (You do not want to alter the template. If you make a mistake that is irreversible you will have to download it again and start from scratch.)

- Open the template in Adobe Photoshop. (A message might come up saying that fonts are missing. Ignore this for now as we will install these fonts soon.)

Now that you have the template open, let's break down what you see.

1. The title is very big. So is the author name. In the age of online shopping, you want your title and name still to be readable when the cover image is seen at thumbnail size. On your left you should see a vertical tool bar. If not, go to *Window* and select *Tools* (right at the bottom of the dropdown menu) and the vertical tool bar will pop up. Look for the little magnifying glass. Click it. Then at the top left of your screen, you will see a magnifying glass with a plus sign and a magnifying glass with a minus sign. Click the magnifying glass with the minus sign until the cover becomes the size of a thumbnail image on Amazon. (If your version of Photoshop doesn't have the magnifying glass with the minus sign, then you can zoom out by going to *View* (top tool bar) and selecting *Zoom Out*.) Can you still read the title and the author name? Yes. This is what you need.

2. Magnify the cover back to its original size (Ctrl + 0). What do you notice about the text? It uses colours that are already present in the cover image. To be safe rather than sorry, I advise you make sure you do not add any colours that aren't already there. Not only do you risk a really ugly colour clash, but you do not want to over-stimulate and confuse the brain of the person looking at it. Just like your story needs to flow and transition smoothly from one sentence and paragraph to the next, so too does the design of your cover. Less is more. Always.

3. What do you notice about the image? There is lots and lots of space. Space is vital for the eye to be attracted to it. If there is too much going on in the image, not only will you struggle to place your title and author name, but it will look too cluttered. People won't know what to focus on. Think of it this way: when there are too many characters introduced at the beginning of a book, not only do you not grasp who is who, but you might get so confused that you stop reading it. The same applies to cover design. There needs to be a clear focus for it to make sense and to hook your reader.

4. The fonts I have used are classic fonts which will translate well for a wide variety of genres. The title and author name use Trajan Pro, and the teaser text is Adobe Garamond Pro (which is also the font I'll advise you to use for your interior). I am a strong advocate for classic fonts, especially when you are just starting out as there is very little room for error. You can download these fonts from ***howtoselfpublishyourbook. net/templates.html*** (remember to enter this password to gain access: selfpub101).

To install the fonts, right-click on the font file and select *Install*. If that option is not available, go to your computer's *Control Panel*, open the *Fonts* folder, and drag and drop all the files into it. They'll start installing immediately. (On some systems these may be labelled differently. The key is to find your *Fonts* folder.)

For a fabulous array of fonts by genre, however, you might like to take a look at this post by Creative Indie: ***creativindie. com/300-fool-proof-fonts-to-use-for-your-book-cover-design-an-epic-list-of-best-fonts-per-genre***. Many fonts are also available for free download. Just Google *Free Fonts*.

5. There is a quarter of an inch of space (0.635 cm) around the margins that is free of text. This is intentional. Even though this is an eBook cover and will not require a bleed (trimming space for the printer), we are going to transfer this design over to your paperback template later on, which *will* require a bleed. So it's best to be prepared.

Right ... let's get cracking.

EBOOK COVER DESIGN STEP-BY-STEP:

1. Find an image that best represents your book. (Do not use the one in the template. Though I have permission to use it, you do not unless you purchase it, and you could get into trouble.) You can find creative commons (copyright-free images) on Flickr: ***flickr.com/creativecommons/***, or a fabulous list of free stock photo sites here: ***bootstrapbay. com/blog/free-stock-photos***.

You can also purchase photos from a stock photo site like Shutterstock.com. This is my favourite because their subscription plans are very affordable and apparently the range of choice is the largest available (over nine million photos and growing).

2. Once you have an image that you're happy with (remember, lots of space!), open the template you saved as your own cover. Make sure the layers panel is open. To open the layers panel, press the F7 key. The layers panel should pop up at the right of your screen. (Refer to Pic. 2a on page 84 for visual.)

See the layer that is highlighted? That's the image that is currently a part of the design. You need to remove that. To remove it, drag and drop it onto the little rubbish bin that is located at the bottom right of the layers panel. You will now see what is represented in Pic. 2b on page 85.

3. You are now going to insert your own image. Make sure the *Background* layer in the layers panel is selected so that the image we insert will be placed below the text. If the *Background* layer isn't selected, all you need to do is click on it once. Go to *File* and select *Place* (or *Place Embedded* in some versions. (Refer to Pic. 2c on page 86 for visual.)

A dialog box will pop up for you to insert a file from your computer. Locate the image you want to use and click *Place*.

Now click the little *Maintain Aspect Ratio* button (circled in Pic. 2d on page 87) and drag the edges of the image until it covers the whole Background area and is placed how you like it.

Note: To remove *Maintain Aspect Ratio* just click the same button again.

4. Now before we work on the text, you need to make sure you don't place any text beyond the bleed line so, when the time comes, you can transfer this design over to your paperback cover with ease. To do this, you need to place some guide lines. It's very easy.

- First, if you don't see a ruler at the top of your screen, go to *View* and then select *Rulers* (Ctrl + R). You will now see a ruler across the top edge and along the left edge.
- Place your cursor over the ruler at the top of your screen, click, hold, and drag. You will see a horizontal line move with your cursor. Place that line a quarter of an inch (0.7 cm) below the top of the image.

- Now do the same thing, but drag the line all the way to the bottom of the image. Place it a quarter of an inch (0.7 cm) above the bottom of the image.
- Now place your cursor over the ruler at the left of your screen. Drag and drop the lines, one at the left and one at the right, a quarter of an inch (0.7 cm) in from the edges. (Refer to Pic. 2e on page 88 for visual.)

Tip: To remove a guide line, click on your guide line and drag it back up to the ruler and it will disappear.

5. Now let's fix your title.

Press T on your keyboard. You will notice that the T in the vertical tool bar to the left is now highlighted. Now click your cursor on YOUR TITLE. The text box it is in will now show up. Press Ctrl + A to select all the text and choose your desired font. (Refer to Pic. 2f on page 89 for visual.)

Keep the text selected and start typing in your book title. If it's too long for the current size of the text box, adjust the size of the text box by dragging it down from the bottom right corner, and/or adjust the size of the actual text by typing in the size you want. (Refer to Pic. 2g on page 90 for visual.) Note that you can have different words as different sizes, too. You just need to select that one word for which you want to change the size.

You will have to play around a bit to get it right depending on how long or short your title is. If you have reduced or enlarged the size of the font considerably, you may also want to alter the space between the letters and/or the words. To do this, select the text again, open the *Character* panel and adjust the numbers until the title looks the way you want it to. (Refer to Pic. 2g on page 90 for visual.) If you can't see the *Character* panel like in the image, go to *Window* (top tool bar) and select *Character* to make it pop up.

Now choose the colour you want your title to be. Remember earlier how I advised you to choose a colour that's already in your image? Let me tell (and show) you how to do that. First, *Select* the entire title (Ctrl + A) again. Then ... (Refer to Pic. 2h on page 91 for visual.)

Step 1: Select your text by highlighting it.
Step 2 in Pic. 2h: Click on this to bring up the colour dialog box.
Step 3 in Pic. 2h: Click the Eyedropper anywhere on the image that has the colour you want to use. You will notice that your text changes the same colour instantly.
Step 4 in Pic. 2h: Click *OK* in the colour dialog box.
Follow the same procedure for your author name and teaser text.

6. To move the position of any text on your cover, click on the layer in the layers panel, then press V on your keyboard. You will notice that the arrow at the very top of the vertical tool bar is now highlighted. You can now either use your mouse to move the text, or the arrows on your keyboard.

Refer to Pic. 2i on page 92 to see my completed cover using the template.

Now that you're done with your front cover, note down the names of the fonts you have used so you don't need to go back in and check while doing your book layout. You're also not going to bother saving this cover as a .jpeg just yet. You could, but it's not necessary. For now, just save it as a .psd and back it up.

3

PREPARE YOUR FRONT/BACK MATTER AND BLURB

I've said a lot about front/back matter and blurbs in *Polish Your Fiction: A Quick & Easy Self-Editing Guide*, but in that book I talk about preparing them editorially. Here I will talk about them from a slightly different perspective, so please don't skip this section.

FRONT/BACK MATTER AND BLURB ORGANIZATION STEP-BY-STEP:

FRONT MATTER

Front matter is subjective and varies from book to book, but I'm going to advise you based on what I would do. The order isn't set in stone, but it's what I think looks best in a paperback.

1. Praise for *Title of Book*

The amount of praise is going to differ depending on the trim size of your book, and the type and size of the font used. So if you intend to put a "Praise" section in the front matter, make sure you collect enough. You can always trim the quotes down too. If you don't have any quotes, or don't want to get quotes from authors or media to put here, don't worry about it. Just start with the next step.

Tip: Here's a great article on endorsement quotes for the cover of your novel: ***selfpublishingadvice.org/should-indie-authors-put-endorsement-quotes-or-puffs-on-self-published-books/***

2. About the Author

A short biography. This speaks for itself really. Many authors put this section in the back, but I think it looks nice at the front in a paperback. (It's different for an eBook, however, which I will talk about later.) Just write something short and sweet, and make sure you include your website URL. Don't include the *http://www*, though, as it looks messy. For example, instead of *http://www.jessicabellauthor.com*, just write *jessicabellauthor.com*.

3. Also by *Author Name*

List all other books you've written under category headings, i.e. "Fiction", "Nonfiction", "Poetry". If you haven't published before, ignore this.

4. Title Page

Your title and author name. Centred and in a large font size preferably. If you have a publisher name you can also put this here. If you look at the title page of this book you'll see how the publisher name is located at the bottom of the page along with its location.

5. Imprint Page (a.k.a. Credit Page, Copyright Page, or Title Page Verso)

The information on this page varies with different publishers and authors, but here is a simple template for you with all the necessary information (replace the bold text with your own):

THE PALACE
Copyright © **2019 Jessica Bell**
All rights reserved.

Published by **Vine Leaves Press 2019**
Melbourne, Victoria, Australia

No parts of this publication may be reproduced, stored in a retrieval system, or transmitted in any form or by any means, electronic, mechanical, photocopying, recording, or otherwise, without the prior written permission of the copyright owner.

This book is sold subject to the condition that it shall not, by way of trade or otherwise, be lent, resold, hired out, or otherwise circulated without the publisher's prior consent in any form of binding or cover other than that in which it is published and without a similar condition including this condition being imposed on the subsequent purchaser. Under no circumstances may any part of this book be photocopied for resale.

This is a work of fiction. Any similarity between the characters and situations within its pages and places or persons, living or dead, is unintentional and co-incidental. *[Remove this bit if your book is nonfiction. If it's a memoir, you may like to insert: Some names and identifying details have been changed to protect the privacy of individuals.]*

Cover photography from **Shutterstock.com**
[Insert additional credits here, if applicable, such as permission to reprint copyrighted material.]

Note: You'll notice that there is no ISBN included here. I'll explain why. As a first-time self-publisher, it's really not necessary to buy your own ISBNs, as the distributors to which you are going to upload your book will provide one for you. And, because you haven't uploaded anything yet, you're not going to know what it is. That's okay. You don't need it. The distributor will include the assigned ISBN in the barcode on the back cover (which they will also provide). So I advise, in order to get your self-publishing feet wet with the least amount of hassle possible, just to ignore this side of business for now. There are a lot of for and against arguments about buying your own ISBNs. It's actually quite a discussion topic amongst self-published authors, so once you've published your first book, and begin to feel comfortable with the process, you can explore the ISBN issue further if you like. But for now, all you need to think is: *ISBNs and barcodes? All sorted.* However, if you would like to purchase your own ISBNs, I'll give you some information about that in Section 7.

6. Dedication

This can be something as simple as *For John*, or it could be a little more detailed and include a reason why. Some people include quotes from other authors that are symbolically relevant to their story. Whatever you do choose to put here, make sure it is centred and the only thing on the page. It's special.

Note: If your book is nonfiction or short stories it will also need a TOC (Table of Contents) in the front of the paperback. Take a look at the front matter of this book for an example.

END MATTER

7. There are a lot of things you can include in the back of your book. Here are some of the popular ones:
- Acknowledgements
- A suggestion to sign up to your author newsletter
- A call to connect with you on your website or other social media platforms
- A call to post a review
- Adverts for your backlist or upcoming titles
- Sample excerpts from your forthcoming titles
- An author interview
- Book club discussion questions

There is no standard way to set any of these things out. Just be creative and do what feels right for you. However, if you're writing nonfiction, there are more rigid rules and other sections you might like to consider adding. If you are writing nonfiction, check out this article: ***https://blog.reedsy.com/front-matter-back-matter-book/***

8. Back Cover Blurb

Write it now. Let it sit. Rewrite it. Let it sit. Have friends read it. Let it sit. Give it time to mature. Proofread it. Proofread it again. Then it will be perfect by the time you are ready to put it on your back cover. There is always something that won't feel right with it, and you will always be given conflicting opinions on it. For me this is the hardest part of this process, so be sure to write it early so you have the chance to make it as perfect as possible. It is after all, the second thing (after the front cover) that potential buyers look at. So please don't rush it!

4

FORMAT YOUR
PAPERBACK INTERIOR

I'm going to assume you know the basics of Microsoft Word as this is the most common word processing program, so my instructions regarding the mechanics of this program's tools are not going to be as in-depth as they were for Adobe Photoshop. If there is anything you don't understand in this section, there are plenty of free online tutorials you can access. The following free tutorials are particularly cool and easy to grasp: *gcflearnfree.org/office*.

Another thing to note: the trim size of this template is 5 x 8 inches (12.7 x 20.32 cm). This is also the trim size of the eBook cover, and will be the trim size of your paperback cover. I have chosen this trim size for the following reasons:

• It's a typical trade paperback size.

- It's not too small and it's not too big. I think it's the most comfortable size to hold when reading.
- All print-on-demand (POD) companies offer this trim size with both white and cream paper.

Note: If you want to change the trim size of the template, all you have to do is go to *Page Layout > Page Setup > Size* and select your size of choice. If you want to read about different trim sizes for various types of books, you can do so here: ***thebookdesigner.com/2010/09/self-publishing-basics-how-to-pick-the-size-of-your-book/***

The margins I have set up in the template should stay the same. Do not change these. These margins are compatible with every POD company out there and will not cause you any problems. I have mirrored the pages and made the outer edges a little wider than the industry standard. The standard 0.5 inch (1.27 cm) margins all around are way too narrow in my opinion, and the text ends up way too close to the spine of the book, which is awkward to read. Trust me, I've been through this.

Once you download the template (see below), you'll notice that it doesn't contain a header. Headers are not necessary and many traditionally published books do not use headers either. Having a header on each page is not going to determine whether your book is professionally formatted. It's simply a matter of style and choice. I have purposely left them out because, again, it's a bit of a learning curve setting them up. Even if I included them in the template, you would still have to learn how to use tools that might make your head spin. My advice is not to bother. If you do want headers, however, you can find a tutorial on how to set them up here: ***gcflearnfree.org/office***.

My instructions on formatting the paperback interior are not fancy. You will end up with a simple, clean, and classy paperback. And really, that is all you need, especially if you're just starting out.

PAPERBACK INTERIOR LAYOUT STEP-BY-STEP:

1. Download the Paperback Interior Template from: ***howtoselfpublishyourbook.net/templates.html*** (remember the password to gain access: selfpub101). Save the .docx file to your desired location and open it. Click *File* and then *Save As* to save it as your own book interior with a different file name.

Note: The default language of the template is set to American English. If you'd like to change this, go to the *Review* tab and then click *Set Language* in the *Proofing* group.

2. If you haven't already downloaded the Adobe Garamond Pro font and you'd like to use it, you can download that from the same link too. (I highly recommend this font. It's easy on the eye, looks professional and classy, isn't too thick or thin. For me, it's the perfect font to use for the interior of a paperback. To install the font, right-click on the file and select *Install*. If you can't see that option, go to *Control Panel*, open the *Fonts* folder, and drag and drop the four Adobe Garamond Pro files into it. They'll start installing immediately. If you can't see the same thing as me, try to locate the *Fonts* folder.

3. Open your paperback interior template and your manuscript. Zoom out so that the template is visible as a whole page on your screen. Copy the entire contents of your manuscript and paste it into your template. Now *Select All*

(Ctrl + A), change the font to Adobe Garamond Pro, 11.5 point, with 0.9 leading, and justify the text. (Refer to Pic. 3a on page 93 for visual.)

Note: If you'd prefer your font to be larger and there to be more space between lines, adjust accordingly.

4. Arrange the front matter as follows and be sure to separate each one with a *Page Break*. Put your cursor at the end of the last word on each page and go to the *Insert* tab, *Pages* group, and click *Page Break* (Ctrl + Return):

Page 1: Praise
Page 2: Blank
Page 3: About the Author
Page 5: Also by [Author Name]
Page 6: Title Page
Page 7: Imprint Page (credits)
Page 8: Dedication
Page 9: Blank
Page 10: Contents Page
Page 11: Blank
Page 12: Start first chapter

I usually make the font size of front matter a lot smaller than the main body. You will notice the same thing in traditionally published books too. My size of choice for the "Praise", "About the Author", and "Also by [Author Name]" sections is 10 pt, and the size for the "Credits Page" is either 8pt or 9pt.

Don't worry about the page numbers showing on any of the front matter at the moment. We will fix that later.

5. Make sure the font of your chapter headings is the same as the title on your cover and that they are centred. You don't *have* to do this, but I highly recommend it. It has to do with visual aesthetics and continuity, which gives your product a professional look. Making the text size bigger is also advised. Choose whatever size you think looks best.

Most professionals would advise you to create *Styles* for your headings so that in the event that you wanted to change the way they looked, you could change them all at once. Setting up *Styles*, however, is a bit of a learning curve, so if you aren't in the mood, or don't have time, just make sure you know exactly how you want your headings to look before fixing them! If you do want to learn about setting up *Styles*, you can find a tutorial at the ***gcflearnfree.org/office*** link I mentioned earlier.

6. Make sure the beginning of each chapter starts on a new page. Do **not** use the *Return* key to get it there. Insert a *Page Break*. If you'd like your chapters to start midway down the page, you can use the paragraph settings. With your cursor on the chapter heading line, go to the *Home* tab and open the *Paragraph* menu. Under the *Spacing* heading you can change the *Before* and *After* settings to whatever you desire. This adds space before and after the selected line, giving a more professional look to the layout of your chapter titles. Apply this same setting to all of your chapter titles.

7. Arrange each section of your back matter on a new page, using a *Page Break*.

Back matter options:

1. Acknowledgments
2. A suggestion to sign up to your newsletter.
3. A call to connect with you on social media.
4. A reminder of where to find more of your books.
5. Some people also like to include a call to post a review, especially at the end of eBooks with a hyperlink that leads directly to their product page.
6. Adverts for your backlist or forthcoming titles
7. Sample excerpts from your forthcoming titles
8. An author interview
9. Book club discussion questions

(The following step is for those who would like to insert images.)

8. To insert images, do not copy and paste as they will diminish in quality.

Note: Make sure all your images are print-ready. They need to be at least 300 DPI, and scaled to size. If you are new to this, please check out these articles for help: *scarlettrugers. com/temp/?p=56* and *blog.klmimages.com/2010/09/ resolution-overview/*

- Place your cursor where you want your image to go.
- Go to the *Insert* tab and click *Picture* in the *Illustrations* group.
- Locate your desired picture and click *Insert*.
- Select the image and navigate to the *Format* tab if you aren't sent there automatically.
- Adjust the size of the image by changing either the *Height* or *Width*. You only need to alter one because the ratio should be locked.

- If the picture doesn't maintain it's ratio, open the *Size* menu and make sure the *Lock aspect ratio* and *Relative to original picture size* options are ticked.(Refer to Pic. 3b on page 94 for visual.)

Note: Unfortunately, on earlier versions of Word you can't see the image changing size while you do this, so it may take a few tries before you get it how you want.

Tip: If you want to move the position of the picture, you can simply drag and drop.

5

PROOFREAD YOUR FORMATTED PAGES

I know you've probably proofread your work a million times and are utterly sick of it, but this step is important because we are now checking for more than textual errors: we're also checking for layout errors.

PROOFREAD YOUR FORMATTED PAGES STEP-BY-STEP:

1. Print out your formatted pages in *Landscape* mode with two book pages per one printed page so it is a similar size to an actual book. The way to do this will differ depending on your printer, so I'm afraid you're going to have to figure this bit out for yourself.

2. Read it through from beginning to end, red pen in hand, and look for the following:

a. typographical errors (you'll be surprised how many you didn't catch before!)
b. inconsistent spacing between lines and words
c. too many hyphenated words in the right margins
d. single words hanging at the end of paragraphs
e. chapter headings that are inconsistent in appearance or numbering
f. page breaks that are not in the right place.

3. Now implement your corrections into the paperback layout .docx. Once you're done with that, make a copy of the file and name it *TITLE_eBook*. You will soon use this file to create your eBook. Your interior layout is probably in perfect shape by now, but if you're in doubt, ask a trusted friend to have a read through it before you move on.

4. Open your paperback layout .docx again and:

• Go to *Word Options*. (Refer to Pic. 4a on page 95 for visual.)
• Go to *Save* and select *Embed fonts*, click *OK*. Close the document. (Refer to Pic. 4b on page 96 for visual.)

Your paperback interior is now ready for the final touches.

6

SAVE YOUR INTERIOR LAYOUT AS A PRINT-READY PDF

Time to warm up the engines of Adobe Acrobat Pro. Unfortunately, the simple Adobe Reader does not have all the functions you need, so you're going to have to embrace Adobe Acrobat Pro. And trust me, as time goes by, and you become more experienced in publishing, you are going to thank your lucky stars that you have this program.

What we are going to do in this section is very simple, but it's essential to have this program because you are also going to need it when the time comes to export your paperback cover as well. All POD companies accept PDFs, so I strongly believe it's in your best interests to have the ability to create PDF documents.

You'll find it also comes in handy for a lot of other things related to your self-publishing business in the future. Not only do POD companies prefer the PDF format for your print-ready files, but so do a lot of real-life human reviewers! Strange, I know. I would much prefer a proper eBook file to transfer to my eReader than read from a PDF, but as experience shows, when I ask what format a reviewer would like my book in, 90% of them ask for a PDF.

SAVE AS A PDF STEP-BY-STEP:

1. Open Adobe Acrobat Pro. Click on *File*, select *Open*, select *All Files* in the dialog box that opens up, and select your edited paperback layout document (not the original template). Once it converts to PDF, save as *TITLE_for_print* in your desired location. (Refer to Pic. 5a on page 97 for visual.)

Note: In newer versions of Word you can save your document as an Adobe PDF from *Save As*. If you prefer to do it this way, go for it. It should automatically open up in Adobe Acrobat Pro if you have that set as the default PDF viewer. If not, you're going to have to open it within the program.

2. Remove page numbers from the desired pages.

- Open your *TITLE_for_print* PDF.
- Go to *View* > *Page Display* > *Two-Up* (or *Two Page View* in some versions). (Refer to Pic. 5b on page 98 for visual.)
- Go to *Tools* > *Edit PDF*. (Refer to Pic. 5c on page 99 for visual.)
- Select the page number you want to delete and hit the delete key. Repeat for subsequent page numbers.

3. Save the file. You now have a print-ready PDF for upload to any POD company that exists.

7

REGISTER WITH DESIRED RETAILERS/DISTRIBUTORS

The reason we are registering with distributors before designing your paperback cover is because there are a few factors which are going to determine the width of your book spine.

Once you register with your POD distributor of choice, you will be able to enter your trim size (the size and shape of your book), page count, and paper colour into their system, and the distributor will create a cover template for you with the necessary spine width according to their specifications.

Before we get you registering, I'd like first to talk about what I believe are your best options. I have used every distributor I'm going to recommend, so I can tell you about these from firsthand experience.

OPTION ONE

You want to spend zero money and can put up with a little bit of uncomplicated, but sometimes time-consuming hassle (especially in the long term when you need to keep track of sales reports and royalties from different places). You're not too fussed about your book only being available from the major retailers (Amazon, Barnes & Noble, Kobo, and iBooks). If this sounds like you, I advise you distribute with:

- Kindle Direct Publishing for Amazon Kindle and print
- Kobo for Kobo, and
- Draft2Digital for iBooks and Nook retailers.

Never heard of these things before? Let me break them down for you.

Kindle Direct Publishing(KDP) is owned by Amazon. It enables you to self-publish in print and electronically for Kindle for free from anywhere in the world. The clincher is that your print book will only be available for sale at Amazon. If you want KDP to distribute to other retailers, such as Barnes & Noble, you will have to register for Expanded Distribution. But books sold via Expanded Distribution channels take a really high percentage of your cut. (In case you don't know, Kindle is an eReader that is exclusive to Amazon.)

Kindle Direct Publishing (KDP) is also owned by Amazon. It enables you to publish your book electronically on Amazon for Kindle from anywhere in the world. (In case you don't know, Kindle is an eReader that is exclusive to Amazon.)

Kobo is an eBook retailer. (It is also the name of their eReading device.) They do not act as a distributor for your eBook. Uploading to Kobo means that your book will be available on Kobo only for readers to purchase from Kobo only. You can upload to Kobo from anywhere in the world without any problems.

Draft2Digital is a distributor who lists your eBook at multiple retailers. Most importantly iBooks (iTunes) and Nook (Barnes & Noble). They also distribute to Kobo and a couple of other less popular sites, but they do take a little cut from your royalties which is why I suggest uploading to Kobo separately. The reason I'm recommending you use Draft2Digital for iBooks and Nook is because these retailers do not allow you to upload your book from anywhere in the world. Well, they do ... but you might not be able to get paid because they do not accept bank accounts from all countries. Being an expat myself, I am aware of these restrictions and think you should know. If you live in the US or UK, however, you will have no problem directly uploading your books to iBooks and Nook, just like I have suggested you do at Kobo.

To register for Option One, go to the following URLs and follow their registration guidelines:

Kindle Direct Publishing: *kdp.amazon.com*
Kobo: *writinglife.kobobooks.com*
Draft2Digital: *draft2digital.com* (for iBooks and Nook + others)
or
iBooks: *itunesconnect.apple.com*
Nook: *nookpress.com*

OPTION TWO

As Amazon is a huge player in this industry, you will benefit from going through Kindle Direct Publishing for eBook regardless, as you will be able to retain a 70% royalty per sale from them. This is a no-brainer for me, and should be for you too.

If you're keen to spend a small set-up fee for minimal hassle in the long run, I advise you register with IngramSpark. IngramSpark doubles as a print and eBook distributor, which saves you an enormous hassle, as you can upload all your files in one place, and all your sales reports and royalties will come from the same place, too. Also, the list of retailers they distribute to is phenomenal, and even though you are going to get the majority of sales via the four main players, the more places your book is available, the better for your visibility online.

To see IngramSpark's distribution partners, visit:
www.ingramspark.com/Portal/distribution_partner

To see the retailers to which IngramSpark distributes, visit:
www.ingramspark.com/Portal/online_retail_partners

IngramSpark has been a lifesaver for me as I'm very busy and I prefer spending a little money for the luxury of saving some time. And it doesn't just save me uploading time. It means I don't have to compile sales reports from multiple places. Everything ends up in one place. Check out Pic. 6a on page 100 for my public endorsement!

However, there is a bit of a downside. You have to provide your own ISBNs to distribute through IngramSpark and they cost money in most countries. I know, I know, I'm sorry. But you want my opinion? If you intend to publish lots of books in the future, and would like to go the IngramSpark no-hassle route, I would buy a batch of 100 ISBNs and be done with having to worry about them for a very long time. The costs vary per country.

Note: If you choose to purchase ISBNs, you will need to assign one ISBN for the paperback and another ISBN for the eBook. So you'll need two ISBNs per book if you go this route. You will not need an ISBN for your Kindle eBook because Amazon will assign it an ASIN, which is an exclusive Amazon Kindle cataloguing number.

Here's a list of where you can purchase ISBNs:

Australia
Thorpe-Bowker: ***www.myidentifiers.com.au***
Prices range from $42 for a single ISBN (plus a $55 registration fee for new publishers) to $2,890 for a block of 1,000.

United Kingdom and Republic of Ireland
Nielsen: ***www.isbn.nielsenbook.co.uk***
Prices start from £120 (plus VAT) for the smallest block.

Canada
Library and Archives Canada: ***bac-lac.gc.ca***
Free! (The way it should be, in my opinion!)

United States

Bowker: ***isbn.org***

Prices start at $125.00 for a single number.

If you're not located in any of the above countries, you can obtain ISBNs from your respective national ISBN registration agency. A directory of ISBN agencies is available here: ***isbn-international.org***

To register for Option Two, go to the following URLs and follow their registration guidelines:

Kindle Direct Publishing: ***kdp.amazon.com***

IngramSpark: ***ingramspark.com***

If you'd like a comprehensive list of distributors, retailers, and assisted self-publishing services, as well as information about specific costs and royalty rates to compare, you might like to check out *Choosing a Self-Publishing Service* by Jim Giammatteo: ***selfpublishingadvice.org/how-to-choose-a-self-publishing-service/***. But if you were looking for this, you probably wouldn't be reading this book!

8

RETRIEVE YOUR PAPERBACK COVER TEMPLATE

You're going to have to get this from either KDP or IngramSpark, depending on which company you've decided to go with.

RETRIEVE YOUR PAPERBACK COVER TEMPLATE FROM KDP STEP-BY-STEP:

1. Go to: ***kdp.amazon.com/en_US/cover-templates***.
You'll see dropdown menus titled *Choose your template*.

2. Fill it in as follows:

Trim Size: *5 x 8 in (12.7 x 20.32 cm)* (if you've chosen a different size for your book, choose that)
Page count: (number of pages)
Paper Color: *Cream* (If you want white, choose *White*, though

cream for novels is more common. *Color* is also an option but will be more expensive and is only needed if you have color images.)

Then click *Download cover template*.

3. Click *Click here to begin Download*. Save to your desired location. Extract the .zip file into the same location. The extracted content will be a folder. Go into that and you will find both a PDF and a PNG file. We are going to use the PDF, so feel free to delete the PNG.

RETRIEVE YOUR PAPERBACK COVER TEMPLATE FROM INGRAMSPARK STEP-BY-STEP:

1. Before you can get your template, you need to enter your title information into their system. So go to your IngramSpark dashboard, click *Add a New Title* and follow the directions. It's a very clear procedure. Once you log in, you will see what to do.

You don't need to fill this in perfectly right now. You can go back to it later to be sure you have filled in your book description, categories, and keywords as best you can. Just make sure the main information, such as ISBN, title, author name, trim size (5" x 8"), interior colour (Black & White), binding type (Paperback > Perfect Bound), and page count is entered correctly. Then save it as a draft.

2. Now go to: ***myaccount.ingramspark.com/Portal/Tools/ CoverTemplateGenerator*** (case-sensitive link) and fill in the form as follows:

13 Digit ISBN: *(Your ISBN)*
Publisher Reference Number: *(Blank)*
Trim Size: *5.000" x 8.000" (203 mm x 127 mm)*
Interior Color and Paper: *Black & White > Creme*
Binding Type: *Paperback > Perfect Bound*
Laminate Type: *Gloss (or Matte if you like)*
Page Count: *(Your page count)*
File Type: *PDF*
Email Address: *(Your email address)*
Confirm Email Address: *(Your email address)*
Price: *(Blank)*
Currency: *(Leave as is)*
Price in Bar Code: *No*

Most of this information should automatically insert itself anyway when you type in the ISBN because you set up the title earlier.

4. You'll get an email in seconds with your PDF template attached. Download it to your desired location.

9

DESIGN YOUR PAPERBACK COVER

Now that you have your paperback template, open up Adobe Photoshop again. I'm going to use the IngramSpark template to demonstrate most of what to do as, generally, the same procedure applies. Where it differs, I will make sure you know.

DESIGN YOUR PAPERBACK COVER STEP-BY-STEP:

1. Open your paperback template. A dialog box that looks something like Pic. 7a on page 101 will pop up.

Make sure all the fields are filled in, the same as in the image. If you're uploading to IngramSpark, make sure it says *CMYK Color* next to *Mode*. If you're uploading to KDP, make sure it says *RGB Color*. Press *OK*.
2. Save as *TITLE_pb_cover* for now in your desired location.

3. For the IngramSpark template, create another layer for your barcode. To do this, copy and paste it in the same position by using the *Rectangular Marquee Tool.*

- Press the M on your keyboard to activate it.
- Drag the cursor around the barcode so that you can see what looks like a perforated line around it.
- Press Ctrl + C and then Ctrl + V. You will see that a new layer pops up in the layers panel.
- Rename that as *Barcode*. You can now move it to any position you like on the back cover. (To rename, just double-click on the text of the layer and it will become editable.)

(Refer to Pic. 7b on page 102 for visual.)

For KDP, you don't need to do anything like this as they will insert the barcode for you after you upload your design. You will see on their template that they have included a yellow rectangle where it will appear. Unfortunately, you can't move the barcode to any other place on the cover with KDP. However, if you'd like to know where it is, so that you are sure you are leaving enough space for it, and/or not covering it up with text, create another layer as described above and then just remove it when you are finished with the design.

The barcode settings with KDP tend to change frequently, so take a look at *selfpublishingadvice.org/* for the latest advice. Also know that KDP adds a barcode to proof copies that is not the final product. It may look larger than normal or a bit distorted, but your final print will have a proper barcode.
4. Now drag horizontal and vertical guide lines so that they line up with the inside and outside of the shading around the

edges and along the spine. (Remember how we did that when designing the eBook cover? If not, see **eBook cover design step-by-step**, Step 4, to remind yourself.) Here, refer to Pic. 7c on page 103 for visual. The lines I have inserted extend beyond the cover.

5. You are now going to insert your eBook design.

- Make sure the *Background* layer in the layers panel is highlighted so that the eBook design will be placed below the barcode. If the *Background* layer isn't highlighted, all you need to do is click on it once.
- Go to *File* and select *Place* (or *Place Embedded* in other versions).
- A dialog box will pop up for you to insert a file from your computer. Locate the Photoshop file (.psd) of your eBook cover and click *Place*.
- Use your keyboard arrows to position the cover on the right side of the template so the text is within the guide lines. (If you're using the IngramSpark template, the image will overlap the edges for now. If you're using the KDP template, you will only have this issue with the left side, where the spine is. Don't worry about this as we'll fix it later.)
- Click the tick in the top tool bar or hit *Enter* to place the image. Your front cover is now inserted and should look something like Pic. 7d on page 104.

6. Now you need to cover the back cover (left side of your template) with a mirror image of your front image.

- Follow the procedure for placing an image, and choose the plain image file (the image you downloaded, not your eBook design).

- Now go to *Edit > Transform > Flip Horizontal*. (Refer to Pic. 7e on page 105 for visual.)
- Align the right side of the image to the left side of your eBook cover image so that it looks like one fluid picture.

AN ALTERNATIVE TO A MIRRORED IMAGE:

If you don't like the look of the mirrored image, you can simply insert a single block of colour on the back.

- Press U on your keyboard to activate the *Rectangle* tool.
- Place your cursor at the top left corner and draw a rectangle over the entire cover.
- To fill with colour, double-click on the coloured section in your new layer—it will be called something like *Shape 1*—and choose your desired colour. Make sure the colour doesn't clash with your front image!
- If your solid colour is placed on top of your front image, all you need to do is reposition the layer in the layers panel (just drag and drop). In other words, the layer at the very top of your layers panel will be placed in front of all the others and the layer at the very bottom of your layers panel will be placed behind all the others.
- It's advisable to extend your front image over your spine to avoid printing inconsistencies. Print-on-demand printers aren't always 100% precise and sometimes the folds of the spine don't fold exactly where indicated on their templates. This means if an image is severely cropped right at the edge of a fold, it might overlap onto the spine by a few millimetres, which can look shoddy. But if your image covers the spine, and is extended by a quarter of an inch or so onto the back cover, you won't have this problem.

If you'd like your front image to fade into the solid colour at the back, do the following:

- In your layers panel, at the bottom, you will see some little icons.
- With your front image selected in the layers panel, click the *Add Layer Mask* icon (it has a grey square with a white circle in the middle).
- See the white square that is linked with your front image layer? Click your cursor on that white square. Then press G on your keyboard. This will activate your *Gradient* tool.
- Now drag your cursor from the left edge of your front cover image to the right edge of your spine. See how it fades? Do this multiple times until the edge of the front image is completely blended in. (Refer to Pic. 7f on page 106 for visual.)

Note: If your mirrored image is not properly fading into the main image, you might have to change the gradient settings. The default gradient will be the *Foreground to Background* gradient. This is the one to use, so if it's not automatically selected you can choose it from the *Gradient picker* at the left of the top toolbar. This also requires that your foreground color is black and your background color is white (these are the little boxes of color at the bottom of the left toolbar). Photoshop should automatically have that all for you, so as long as you haven't used Photoshop before and made changes to those tools, everything should work as planned.

7. If you've chosen to use the mirrored image and it doesn't completely cover the left side of your template, you're going to have to fix that. For example, see how in Pic. 7g on page 107 you can still see a little bit of the template background? Even though this is the trim area and will most likely be cut off, it's better to be safe than sorry. If the book gets printed slightly off centre (which can happen with POD on the rare

occasion), you may end up with a light blue line (or a red one if you're working with the KDP template) at the back edge of your book.

So use the same technique for copying the barcode to select a thin slither of the back image:

- Press M on your keyboard to activate the *Rectangular Marquee Tool*.
- Drag the cursor around the edge of the back image so that you can see what looks like a perforated line around it.
- Press Ctrl + C and then Ctrl + V. You will see that a new layer pops up in the layers panel.
- Rename that layer *Back slither* so you don't get confused about what it is.
- Now mirror that back slither with your main back image: *Edit > Transform > Flip Horizontal.*
- Use your keyboard arrows to adjust the placement as necessary.

8. Now you need to merge all these images to make them one.

- In the layers panel, click on your eBook cover layer so it is highlighted.
- Now hold down the Ctrl key and click on your back slither layer and your cover image layer (or your solid colour layer). All three layers should now be highlighted.
- Hold your cursor over one of your selected layers, right click and select *Merge Layers*. (Refer to Pic. 7h on page 108 for visual.)

The name of that layer will change once merged, so rename it if you like. I've renamed mine as *cover image*.

9. You may skip this step if you're using the KDP template. If you're using the IngramSpark template, we're going to trim the edges of your cover image so that it doesn't overlap the edges into the transparent area. It's very important that you do this as IngramSpark make it very clear in their guidelines that nothing should be placed outside of the shaded areas.

- Press E to activate the *Eraser* tool.
- Choose the *Soft Round 100 Pixels* brush. (Refer to Pic. 7i on page 109 for visual.)
- Make sure your cover image layer is selected in the layers panel.
- Hold down the Shift key (it will keep your cursor moving in a straight line), and drag the cursor along each edge of your cover to erase any overlapping image. You should only erase the image up to the outer guide line. (Refer to Pic. 7j on page 110 for visual.)

10. To add text to the back of your cover:

- Press T and insert a text box where you want the text to appear.
- Copy and paste your back cover text into the text box and adjust the font type, size, and alignment to however you want it to look. You can locate these in the tool bar at the top of your screen. If you want justified text, you can change that in the paragraph panel on the right. (Refer to Pic. 7k on page 111 for visual.)
- Make sure the text is centred between the inner guide lines and does not overlap the barcode. If your text box is the size you want it, but isn't centred properly, all you have to do is click outside of your text box, press V, and use your keyboard arrows (or drag it with your mouse) to move it to where you want it.

If you can't read your text properly, here are a couple of solutions:

- For dark text on a primarily light background, create an *Outer Glow*.
- For light text on a primarily dark background create a *Drop Shadow*.

How to create an *Outer Glow*:

- Select your text layer.
- At the bottom of the layer window, select the *fx* dropdown menu and select *Outer Glow*. (Refer to Pic. 7l on page 112 for visual.)
- Play around with the *Spread* and *Size* under *Elements* until it looks the way you want it to. (Make sure *Preview* is selected so you can see the difference as you play.)
- Click *OK*.
- Now double-click on the actual text that reads *Outer Glow*, which will appear under your text layer if you want to make further changes. (Refer to Pic. 7m on page 113 for visual.)

How to create a *Drop Shadow*:

- Follow the same procedure for *Outer Glow*, but select *Drop Shadow* instead.
- To make sure the shadow appears evenly behind the words (rather than at an angle), under *Structure* set the *Angle* at 90 degrees. Play around with the *Spread* and *Size* until it looks the way you want it to. You may also like to set the *Distance* to 0, but the difference in appearance from the default is minimal. (Refer to Pic. 7n on page 114 for visual.)

Feel free to add any other information you'd like to the bottom left hand corner next to the barcode. I often add my publisher logo and a bit of copyright information. But it's totally up to you. I've seen others add their website URL, which I also think is a good idea. You might also like to have a look at the back of traditionally published books for ideas. (Refer to Pic. 7o on page 115 for visual.)

11. To add text to your spine, follow the general text-box procedure. Don't worry that it's not placed over your spine to begin with. Just add it horizontally to anywhere on your cover and alter the text to the way you want it to look. To rotate your text, go to *Edit > Transform > Rotate 90° CW*. (Refer to Pic. 7p on page 116 for visual.)

Move the text onto the spine. Make sure it's centred between the inner guide lines. (Refer to Pic. 7q on page 117 for visual.)

12. One more thing before you shut down Adobe Photoshop: you need to save it as a print-ready PDF.

- Make a copy of your file and save it as *TITLE_pb_cover_flat*.
- Go to *Layer > Flatten Image*. (Refer to Pic. 7r on page 118 for visual.)
- Go to *File > Save As*.
- In the dialog box, change the name of your file to *YourISBN_cov* for IngramSpark, or keep it as is for KDP. Select *Photoshop PDF* in the dropdown menu and click *Save*. If a message pops up telling you about settings being overridden, just click *OK*. (Refer to Pic. 7s on page 119 for visual.)

Note: For clarity consider naming your files with your ISBN, the distributor they are intended for, and whatthe file contains *YourISBN_IngramSpark_txt*.

•   Now a *Save Adobe PDF* dialog box will pop up. In the Adobe PDF Preset field, make sure you select *PDF/X-1a:2001* and click *Save PDF*. (Refer to Pic. 7t on page 120 for visual.)

13. Now open your eBook cover in Photoshop, flatten it (*Layer > Flatten Image.*), name it *TITLE_eBook_cover_flat* and save it as a *.JPEG*. You will need a .jpeg of your eBook cover for retailers and for when you prepare your retail-ready eBook file.

10

FORMAT YOUR EBOOK INTERIOR

There are so many different techniques for creating eBook files—and I have tried almost every single one of them. There are many "easy" ways to create eBook files from a Word document, but you know what? I don't trust them, because every single time I have done that, I have run into problems. Sometimes the formatting doesn't look the way it's supposed to, sometimes the distributor rejects the file because there is something wrong with the coding that you can't see, or sometimes one of the retailers rejects it for a similar reason. So ... after many years of experimenting with different techniques, I have finally come across the best and most foolproof technique there is which will guarantee a completely clean and error-free eBook file that you can upload everywhere without a glitch.

I must bow and offer a huge thanks to Guido Henkel's *Zen of eBook Formatting*, a book which shows you step by step how to create an eBook using an HTML editor (Notepad++). Don't worry, I'm not going to make you read it! (Though I suggest you do at some point if you want to start doing more fancy things with your books.) What I'm going to do is give you a nice, clean template to work from, into which you can just copy and paste specific sections of your manuscript after a few tweaks in the Word document. In the following section, I will then tell you how to convert your HTML file into an ePub file which you will be able to upload to every single distributor and/or retailer available to you—including Kindle!

FORMAT YOUR EBOOK STEP-BY-STEP:

1. Open your file *TITLE_eBook* in Word. We need to add a few small codes to your Word .docx to make sure it all translates over to HTML without any fuss.

2. Identify and format all words in italics.

- Click Ctrl + H.
- In the *Find what* field, insert your cursor, click on *More* and then click on *Format* at the bottom of the dialog box.
- In the dropdown menu select *Font*.
- Another dialog box will pop up. In the *Font style* field, choose *Italic* and click *OK*. (Refer to Pic. 8a on page 121 for visual.)
- Now insert *<i>^&</i>* in the *Replace* field and click *OK*. (Refer to Pic. 8b on page 122 for visual.)
- All words in italics in your Word .docx will now look like this: <i>*words in italics*</i>
- Do the same for your bold text, but use *^&* instead of *<i>^&</i>*.

3. Replace all en-dashes and/or em-dashes with the correct HTML code to be sure they appear correctly.

- In the *Find and Replace* dialog box insert the en-dash (–), or em-dash (—), whichever one you use, into the *Find* field.
- Insert *–* (en-dash) or *—* (em-dash) into the *Replace* field and press *OK*.

4. Locate any accented letters, for example the *é* in *café*, and replace them with the correct HTML code. You can find a great list here: ***starr.net/is/type/htmlcodes.html***

5. If you have images in your manuscript, remove them. In their place, type the following:
<img src="filename.jpg"/>.
If you want your images centred, add:
* <img src="filename.jpg"/> * instead.

Note: Make sure you actually replace *filename* in the above with the exact name of your image file. Also make sure to use JPEGs. It won't work with PNGs.

6. Download the *eBook_Interior_Template.html* from ***howtoselfpublishyourbook.net/templates.html*** (password to gain access: selfpub101). Make a copy of the template and save one copy in another folder so you can keep using it for your future books.

7. Open the template in *Notepad++*, which is your HTML editing program and *Save as* the title of your book. (If you have images in your book, be sure to put all your images in the same folder as this file.)

You will see a whole lot of coding at the top, which you most likely will not understand in the slightest. Just ignore all of that. I have inserted it to make your life easy. (If you'd like to understand what it all means, read Guido Henkel's, *Zen of eBook Formatting*.)

Tip: To see what the formatting will actually look like, double-click on the HTML file in its folder to open it in your Internet browser. You can decrease the size of your browser window to that of an eReader screen to get a better idea of appearance. Please note, however, that page breaks do not show up in your browser. Also, when you make changes to the HTML file in Notepad++, you will need to click *Save* and then refresh your browser for the changes to take effect there.

8. Scroll down to where you can see *YOUR TITLE, YOUR NAME*, and *Dedication*. From this point on, any text that is black, can be replaced. While you're there, replace *YOUR TITLE, YOUR NAME*, and *Dedication* with the correct text. Be very careful not to remove any of the coding on the left and right of the text. If even one character/symbol is removed, the formatting will be removed also. (Refer to Pic. 8c on page 123 for visual.)

9. Now scroll down a little further, where you will see *Chapter 1*. You can leave that as is if you're happy with the beginning of your chapters starting like that. I've numbered each consecutively all the way up to 25. If your chapters have titles instead of numbers, just replace the text with what you want it to be. Do not mess with what is before and after the text on this line, as it is formatted to have special qualities, such as larger font and a page break before it.

10. If you have more than 25 chapters, all you have to do is copy and paste extra segments after Chapter 25 and insert new numbers. The text you should copy and paste, looks like Pic. 8d on page 123.

Similarly, if you have fewer than 25 chapters, you can remove those that you don't need.

11. If you'd like to add a subtitle, paste your subtitle over the text that says *Your Chapter Title. Remove this whole line if you don't have one. If you'd like to use the title instead of "Chapter 1", insert it in the line above.* If you don't have any need for this, remove all the lines that look like this, including the coding before and after them. (Refer to Pic. 8e on page 124 for visual.)

12. Now replace all instances of *The first paragraph of your chapter goes here* with the first paragraph of each chapter. I have formatted this paragraph not to be indented, and to automatically turn the first line into SMALL CAPS. The number of words on the first line will change when a reader alters the font and text size on their eReading device. The formatting I have here will ensure that the words *only* on the first line of the first paragraph will be capitalized.

13. Now replace all instances of *<p>The rest of your chapter goes here.</p>* with the rest of each chapter. The codes *<p>* and *</p>* mark the opening and closing of each paragraph. I'm making you delete these bits too so that they don't double up in the next step.

14. We now have to insert *<p>* and *</p>* at the beginning and end of each paragraph. Don't freak out. You don't have to do this manually.

- Select all the paragraphs in Chapter 1 (from paragraph two onwards).
- Press Ctrl + H for the *Find and Replace* dialog box to pop up.
- Make sure *Regular expression* is selected (bottom left of dialog box) and insert the following (Refer to Pic. 8f on page 125 for visual.):
  Find what: ^(.+)$
  Replace with: <p>$1</p>
- Click *Replace All*.

All your paragraphs will now have a *<p>* at the beginning and *</p>* at the end. It's necessary for these to be there so that each paragraph, from paragraph two onwards, starts on a new line and is indented. (Refer to Pic. 8g on page 126 for visual.)

Repeat Step 14 for each chapter.

15. Now complete the end matter with the relevant information using the skills you have learned in Steps 7–14. Remember, only replace text that is black.

11

EXPORT YOUR HTML (EBOOK) TO A RETAIL-READY FILE

Terms you need to know first:

.mobi: This is the name of the eBook format that Amazon uses. There is no other eBook retailer, except for Amazon, that uses this format.

.ePub: This is the name of the eBook format used for the majority of other eBook retailers, such as Barnes & Noble (Nook), Kobo, and Apple (iBooks).

Even though the eBook format on Amazon is .mobi, they still allow you to upload an .ePub file which they will convert for you. And seeing as every other eBook retailer and distributor on the planet requires an ePub file, there is no reason why you need to export your eBook in any other format. So that's what we're going to do—export your HTML file into an .ePub file which you can upload to all retailers.

First, if you haven't done so already, download Calibre (it's free) here: ***calibre-ebook.com***

EXPORT TO EPUB STEP-BY-STEP:

1. Open Calibre and add the HTML file you created in the last section. You can find the *Add Book* button at the top left of the screen. (Refer to Pic. 9a on page 127 for visual.)

2. Now click *Edit Metadata*, the button to the right of *Add Book*. A dialog box will pop up. Fill in the following details:

Title: *Your Title* (e.g. The Palace)
Title sort: *Your Title* (e.g. Palace, The)
Author(s): *Your Name* (e.g. Jessica Bell)
Author sort: *Name, Your* (e.g. Bell, Jessica)
Comments: *your book description*

Also click the *Browse* button and add your front cover. Click *OK*. (Refer to Pic. 9b on page 128 for visual.)

3. Now click on your book in the list so it's highlighted and then click *Convert books*, the button to the right of *Edit Metadata*. A dialog box will pop up. In the upper right hand corner you need to select the eBook format you want to export in. Make sure you select EPUB, which is the first option in the dropdown menu. (Refer to Pic. 9c on page 129 for visual.)

4. Don't press *OK* yet. We need to do more here. Click on *Structure Detection* on the left. In this section, you need to leave everything as it is except set *Chapter mark* to *None*. The reason we are setting it to none is because the formatting of the HTML file will already tell Calibre to do what we want. (Refer to Pic. 9d on page 130 for visual.)

5. Now click on *Table of Contents* on the left. What we are going to do here is tell Calibre to use our HTML formatting to create a hyperlinked TOC (contents page) and insert it in the finished product. Ignore everything in this dialog box except:

- Enter in the *Level 1 TOC (XPath expression)* field, the following: *//h:p[re:test(@class, "chap", "i")]*
- Select *Manually fine-tune the TOC after conversion is completed.* (Refer to Pic. 9e on page 131 for visual.)

6. Next up, click on *EPUB Output*. Select the following:

- *Preserve cover aspect ratio*
- *Insert inline Table of Contents*
- *Put inserted Table of Contents at the end of the book.*(Refer to Pic. 9f on page 132 for visual.)
- Click *OK*.

7. You will notice at the bottom right-hand corner that Calibre is generating your ePub. Once the hamster wheel has finished spinning, a dialog box will pop up, which will allow you to look over your Table of Contents.

If everything looks fine, click *OK*. If there is anything you don't want included, such as chapter sub-headings that may have popped up, all you need to do is click on the text you want to remove and then click on *Remove this entry*. Do this for all the entries you don't want visible in your Table of Contents and then click *OK*. (Refer to Pic. 9g on page 133 for visual.)

8. Now you're ready to save your ePub file to your computer. Click on *Save to disk* (located in the top toolbar), select which folder you want to save it in on your computer and then you're done!

Once it's saved, you will notice there are quite a few different files that have been saved. The only file you will need to upload to retailers/distributors is the ePub file. (Refer to Pic. 9h on page 134 for visual.)

12

UPLOAD YOUR PAPERBACK AND EBOOK TO RETAILERS/DISTRIBUTORS

I don't need to tell you how to do this because each retailer/ distributor I've suggested you use is really user-friendly. They give you step-by-step instructions on how to upload and publish your book, so I would really just be repeating myself here if I outlined the steps for you. Though I do want to mention that when a distributor asks for an eBook cover file, they mean the JPG of just the front cover, not the PDF of the entire cover.

I would also like to stress that you choose the appropriate categories and keywords for your book. For two extremely thorough and useful articles about this, and what they mean for you, go to: *janefriedman.com/2013/07/08/optimizing-metadata* and *ingramspark.com/blog/book-metadata-tips-for-indie-authors*

I would also like to advise you to preview what your book will look like on a Kindle and an ePub Reader.

To preview what it looks like on an ePub reader, you can download Adobe Digital Editions (for free): ***adobe.com/ solutions/ebook/digital-editions/download.html***

You can preview it on Kindle once you've uploaded it to Kindle Direct Publishing as they have an inbuilt previewer you can use before you hit that publish button.

Can you believe you're almost done?

Do you realize you're going to have a published book within the next 24 hours?

Congratulations!!!

13

NEED EXTRA SELF-PUBLISHING ADVICE?

Check out Independent Publishing Assistance.

"We want to help you shine the way you deserve to shine."

Combined, our team of thirty publishing experts have over 300 years of publishing experience from the 21st century. That's a helluvalotta modern-day publishing expertise. And the best part about us is ... we're all authors too. This means we 'get' you.

The core members of our team are hybrid authors. This means that we know all about traditional publishing and self-publishing and we are advocates of both. Some members of our team are published by Simon & Schuster, Zondervan, Pen and Sword, and Hodder. But we believe there is no taking sides in this business. We are all authors no matter what and support all publishing paths.

Visit for more information: ***www.indiepublishingassist.com***

14

RECOMMENDED NEXT STEPS

Join the Alliance of Independent Authors for education, advocacy, help, great discounts on services, and networking with other self-published authors: *allianceindependentauthors.org*. As a member, you get great discounts with IngramSpark. You also get 10% off a professional book cover design from me.

Start a website/blog, join Twitter and Facebook and start networking with potential readers. You can get some great advice here: *thecreativepenn.com/marketing*

Consider releasing your title as an audio book: *acx.com*

Write and publish another book! The best way to gain traction in this industry is to have a backlist of books.

Start building it. Now.

ACKNOWLEDGEMENTS

This is the part where I'm supposed to thank everyone that helped me with this book. So here goes ...

Thank you to everyone who helped me with this book.

Okay, seriously now ...

Many thanks go to the authors who were my guinea pigs and offered invaluable feedback on an early draft of this book: Glynis Smy, Terry Freedman, and Misha Gericke. And thanks to Kevin Booth who copyedited the 1st Edition of this book on such short notice.

Of course, I mustn't forget Amie McCracken, an inspiring young woman and powerhouse, who not only helped revise this 2nd Edition, but who's also been my go-to editor, typesetter, and eBook formatter, since we met in 2011. My life would be in a shambles without her. Thank you for being such a great colleague and friend, Amie.

If you found this book helpful, it would be extremely appreciated if you could post a review at the retailer you purchased it from.

Interested in my upcoming titles?
*You can sign up for my newsletter at **jessicabellauthor.com** to stay up-to-date.*

Independent Publishing Assistance

All your book production needs at your fingertips.

www.indiepublishingassist.com

PICTURE AIDS

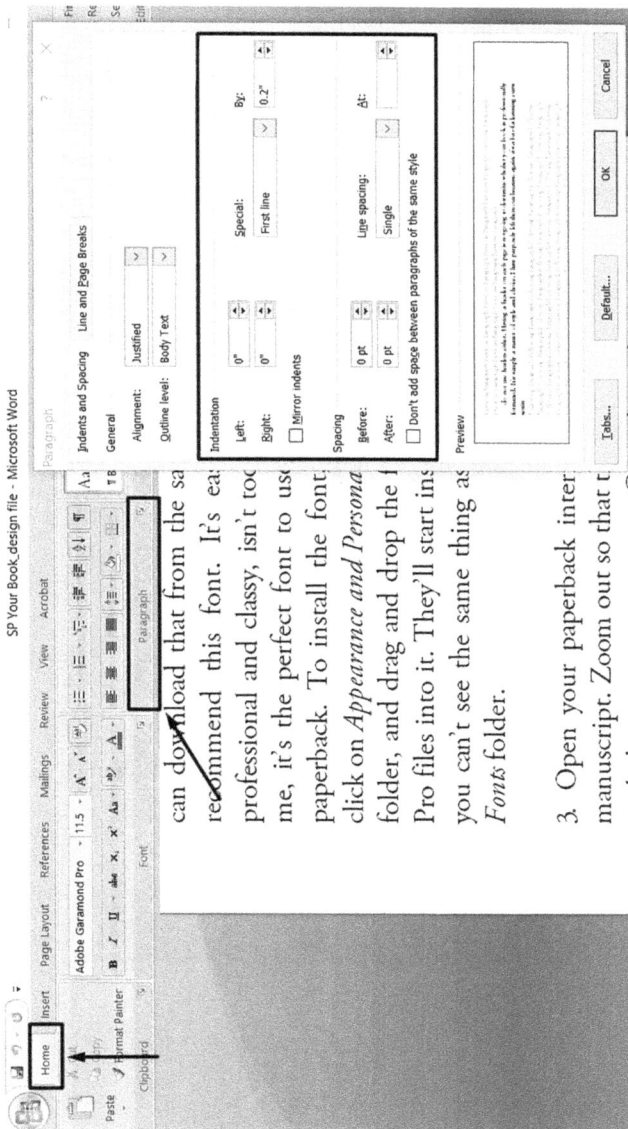

can download that from the sa

recommend this font. It's ea:

professional and classy, isn't too

me, it's the perfect font to use

paperback. To install the font

click on *Appearance and Persona*

folder, and drag and drop the f

Pro files into it. They'll start ins

you can't see the same thing as

Fonts folder.

3. Open your paperback inter

manuscript. Zoom out so that t

Pic. 1a

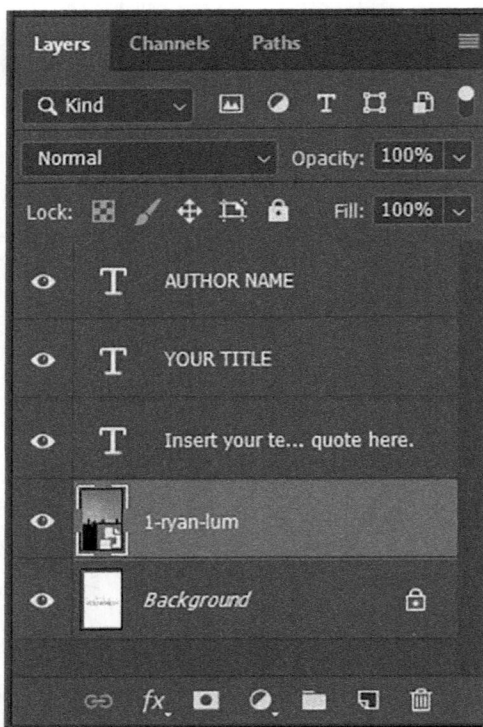

Pic. 2a

Pic. 2b

Pic. 2c

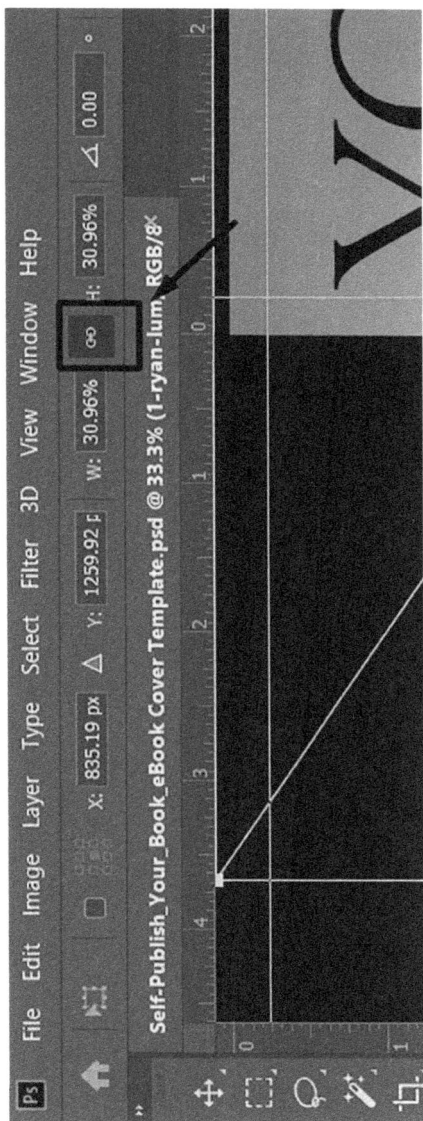

Pic. 2d

Pic. 2e

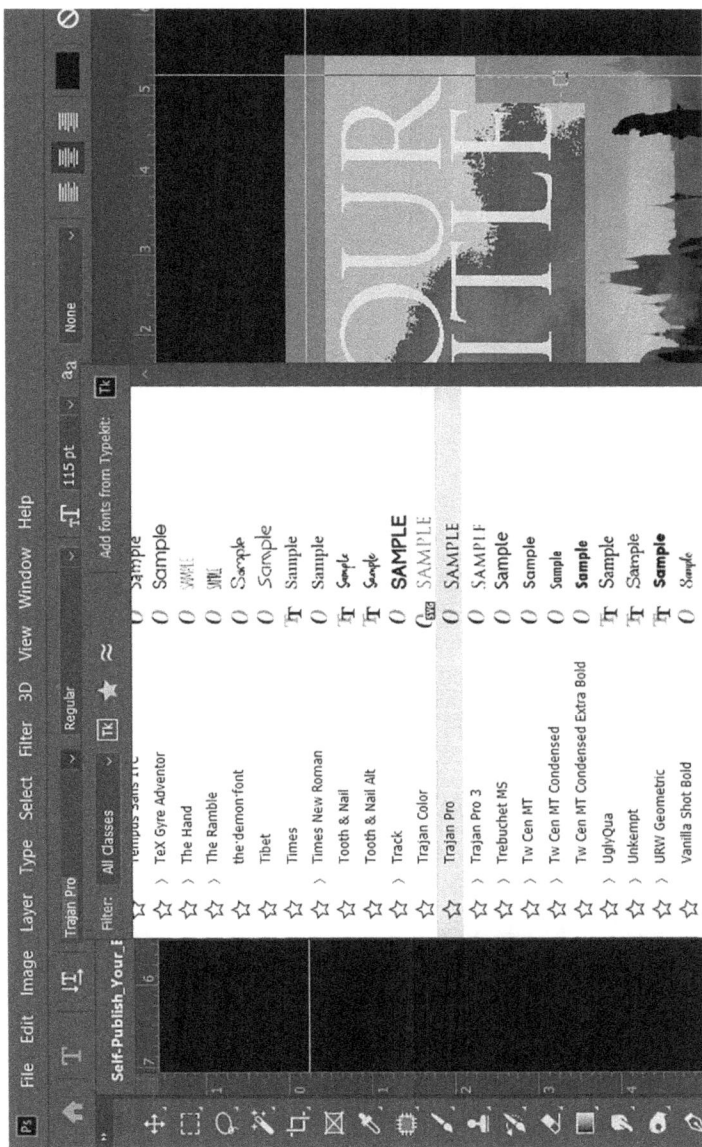

Pic. 2f

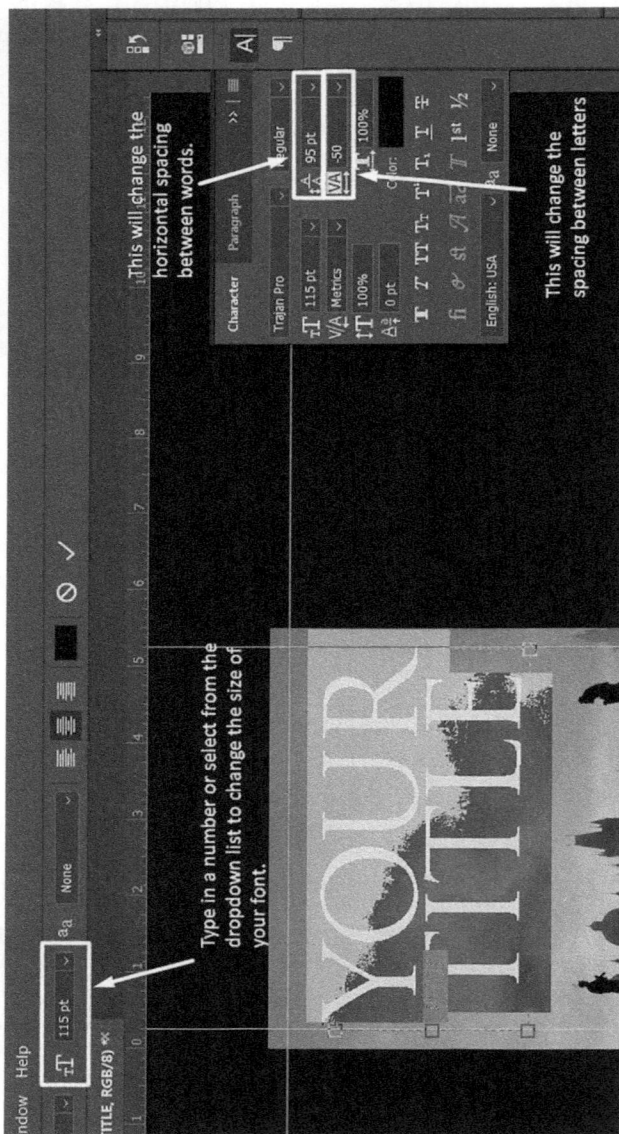

Type in a number or select from the dropdown list to change the size of your font.

This will change the horizontal spacing between words.

This will change the spacing between letters.

Pic. 2g

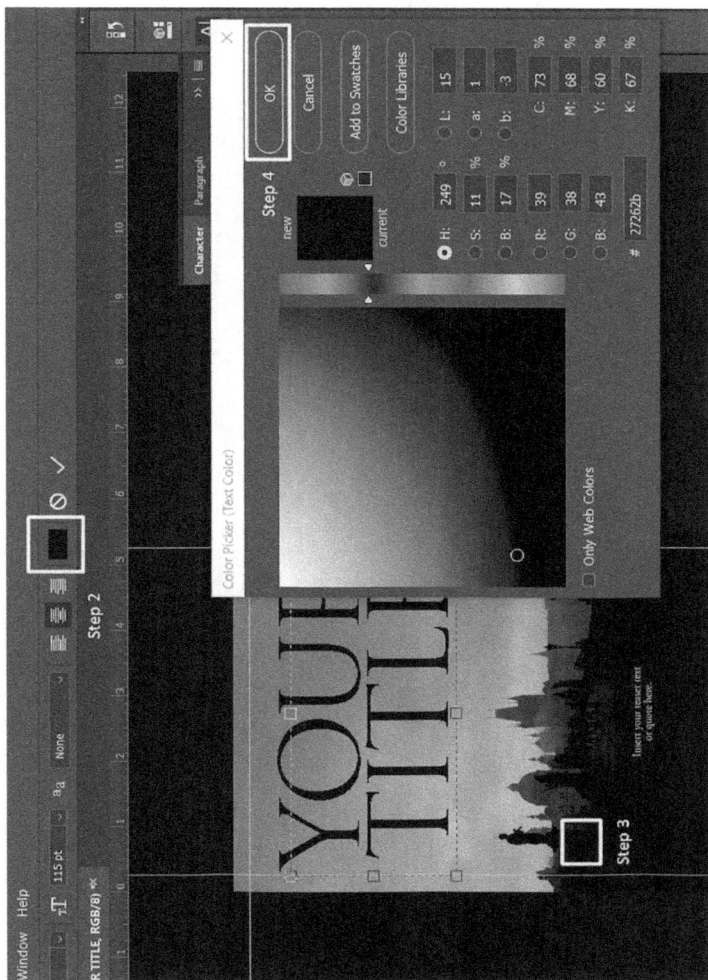

Pic. 2h

THE PALACE

One death.
Five questions.
A million possibilities.

JESSICA BELL

Pic. 2i

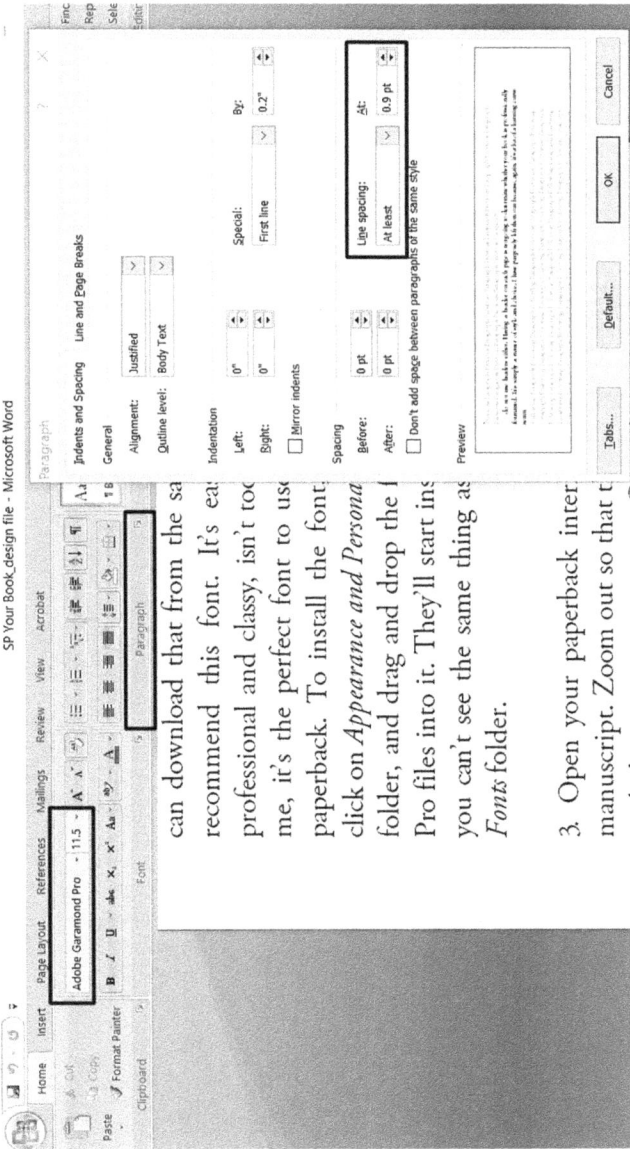

SP Your Book_design file - Microsoft Word

can download that from the sa
recommend this font. It's ea
professional and classy, isn't too
me, it's the perfect font to us
paperback. To install the font
click on *Appearance and Persona*
folder, and drag and drop the
Pro files into it. They'll start ins
you can't see the same thing as
Fonts folder.

3. Open your paperback inter
manuscript. Zoom out so that t

Pic. 3a

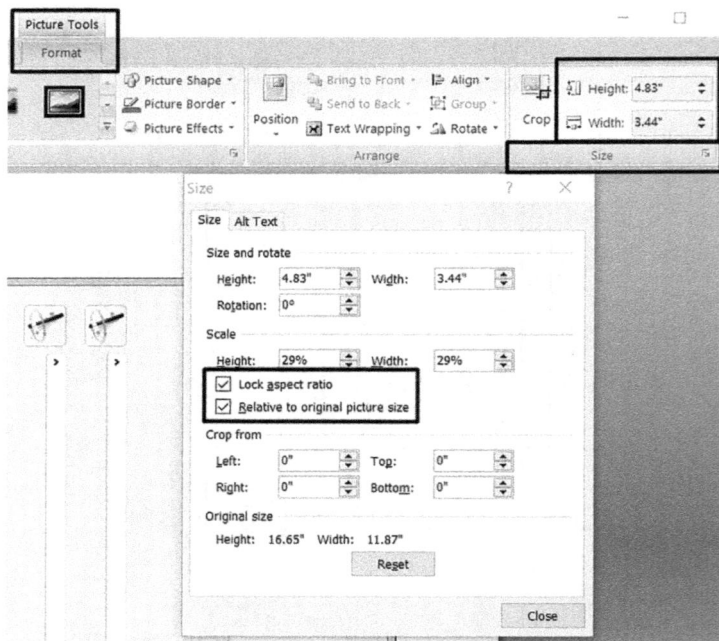

Pic. 3b

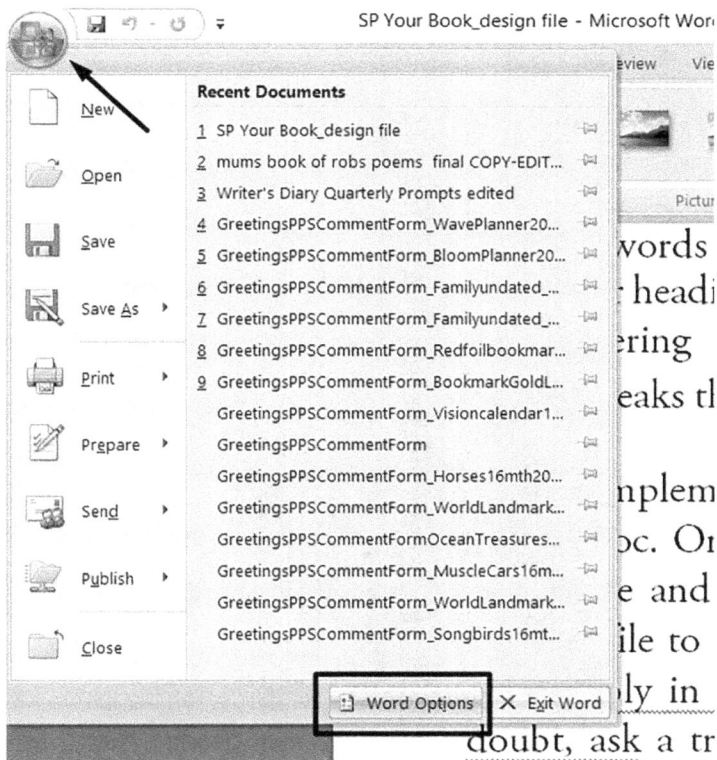

Pic. 4a

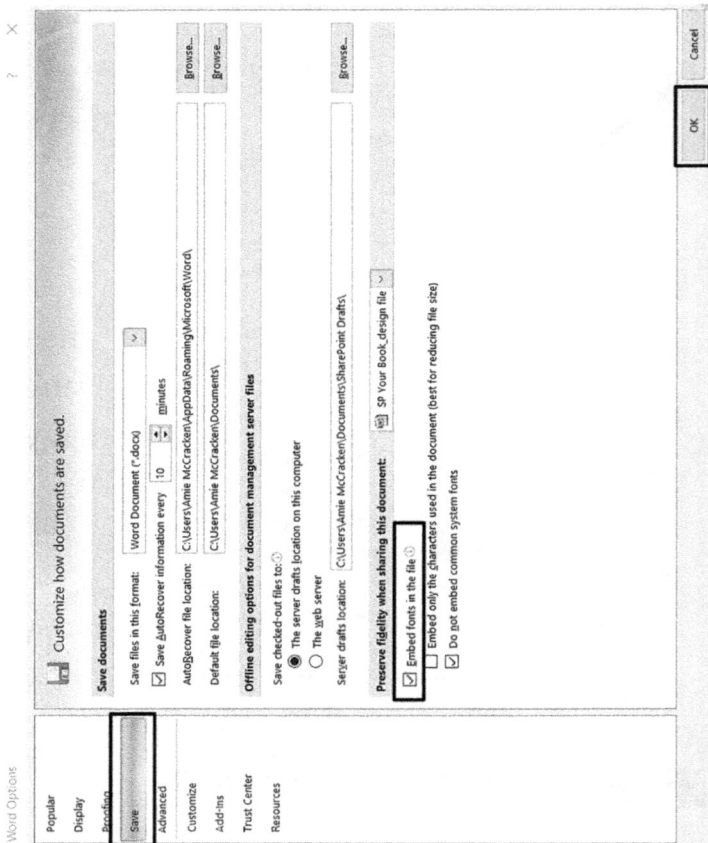

Word Options

Popular
Display
Proofing
Save
Advanced
Customize
Add-Ins
Trust Center
Resources

Customize how documents are saved.

Save documents

Save files in this format: Word Document (*.docx)

☑ Save AutoRecover information every 10 minutes

AutoRecover file location: C:\Users\Amie McCracken\AppData\Roaming\Microsoft\Word\   Browse...

Default file location: C:\Users\Amie McCracken\Documents\   Browse...

Offline editing options for document management server files

Save checked-out files to:

◉ The server drafts location on this computer
○ The web server

Server drafts location: C:\Users\Amie McCracken\Documents\SharePoint Drafts\   Browse...

Preserve fidelity when sharing this document: 📄 SP Your Book_design file

☑ Embed fonts in the file
  ☐ Embed only the characters used in the document (best for reducing file size)
  ☑ Do not embed common system fonts

OK   Cancel

Pic. 4b

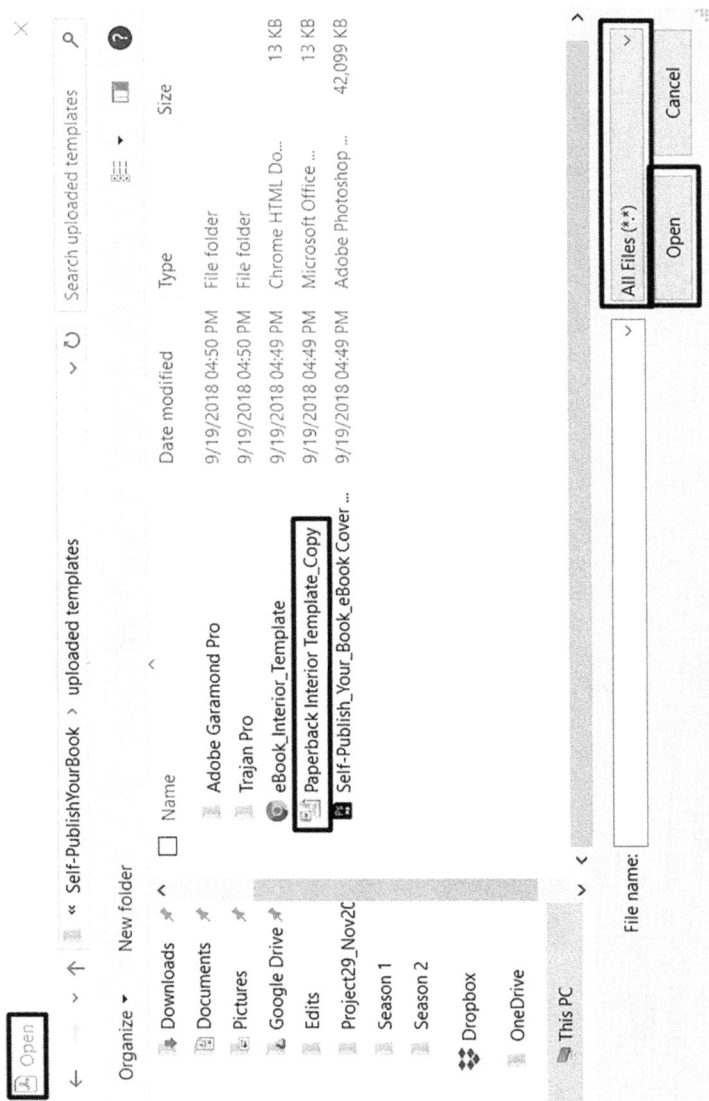

Pic. 5a

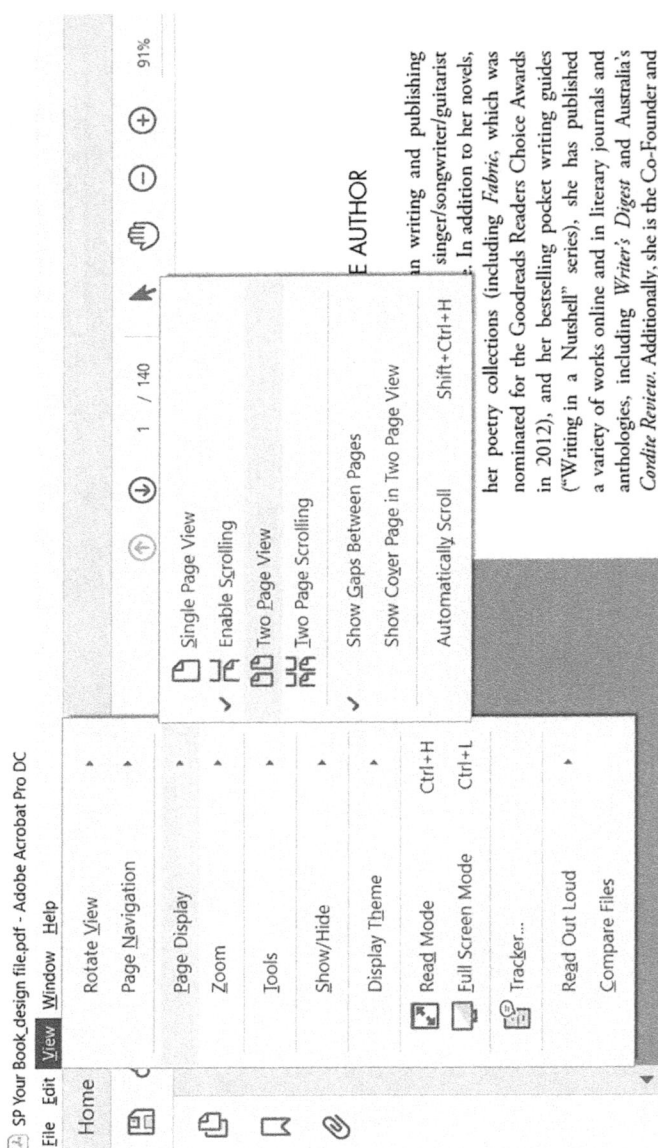

SP Your Book_design file.pdf - Adobe Acrobat Pro DC

File Edit View Window Help

Home

Rotate View

Page Navigation

Page Display

Zoom

Tools

Show/Hide

Display Theme

Read Mode   Ctrl+H

Full Screen Mode   Ctrl+L

Tracker...

Read Out Loud

Compare Files

Single Page View

Enable Scrolling

Two Page View

Two Page Scrolling

Show Gaps Between Pages

Show Cover Page in Two Page View   Shift+Ctrl+H

Automatically Scroll

1 / 140   91%

E AUTHOR

n writing and publishing singer/songwriter/guitarist s. In addition to her novels, her poetry collections (including *Fabric*, which was nominated for the Goodreads Readers Choice Awards in 2012), and her bestselling pocket writing guides ("Writing in a Nutshell" series), she has published a variety of works online and in literary journals and anthologies, including *Writer's Digest* and Australia's *Cordite Review*. Additionally, she is the Co-Founder and

Pic. 5b

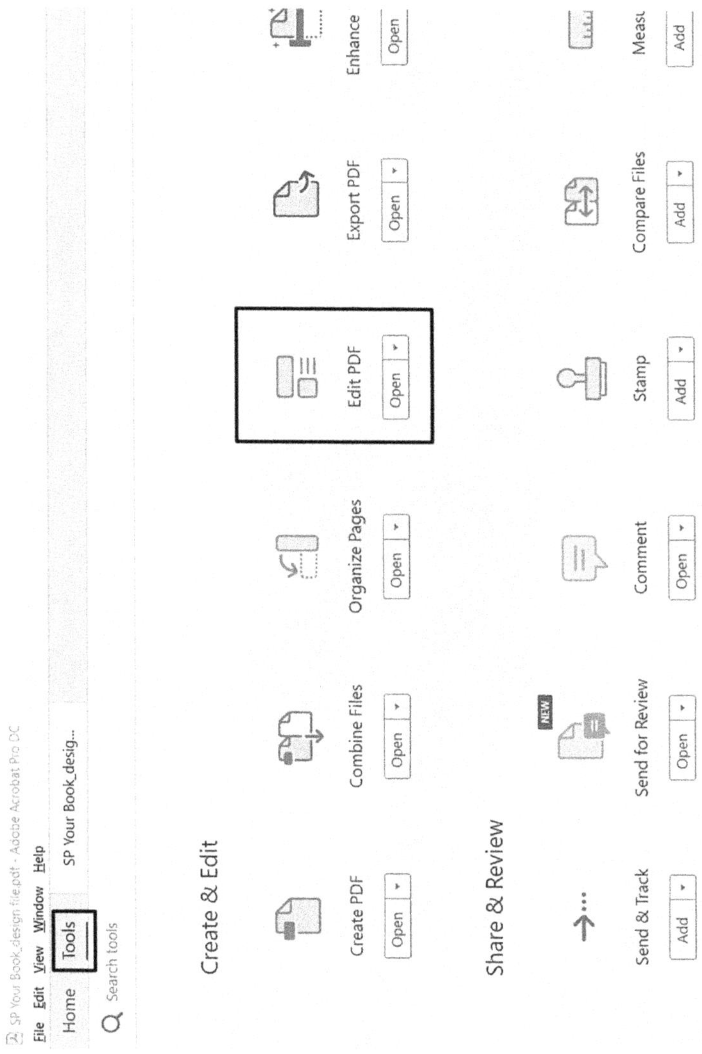
SP Your Book_design file.pdf - Adobe Acrobat Pro DC
File Edit View Window Help
Home
Tools
SP Your Book_desig...
Search tools
Create & Edit
Create PDF
Open
Combine Files
Open
Organize Pages
Open
Edit PDF
Open
Export PDF
Open
Enhance
Open
Share & Review
Send & Track
Add
NEW
Send for Review
Open
Comment
Open
Stamp
Add
Compare Files
Add
Measu
Add

Pic. 5c

IngramSpark

Access your Account   Email Address   Password   Log In
Forgot your password?

Why IngramSpark   How it Works   Costs & Revenue   Global Reach   Products & Services   Help

Don't have an IngramSpark Account?

It's FREE and easy.

Create New Account

- OR -

Have Questions?

A no-fuss, **user-friendly** system. IngramSpark is honestly a **life-saver** and a **time-saver**! I wouldn't be able to publish without them.

Jessica Bell,
author of *Polish Your Fiction:
A Quick & Easy Self-Editing Guide*

E-BOOK DISTRIBUTION
Connect your e-book to retailers— big, small, mainstream, and indie.

PRINT ON DEMAND
Beautiful books printed when you need them and shipped directly to you or your customers.

COLOR PRINTING
Stunning print quality in vibrant color at prices comparable to black-and-white.

GLOBAL REACH
Make your book accessible to more than 39,000 booksellers, online retailers, and libraries worldwide.

Pic. 6a

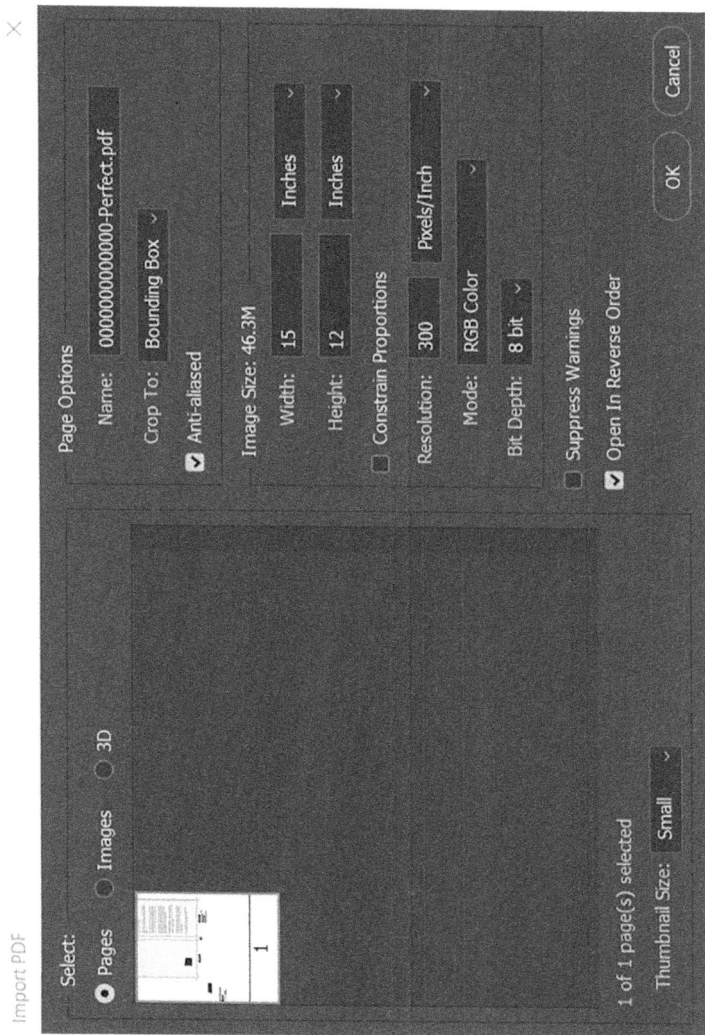

Pic. 7a

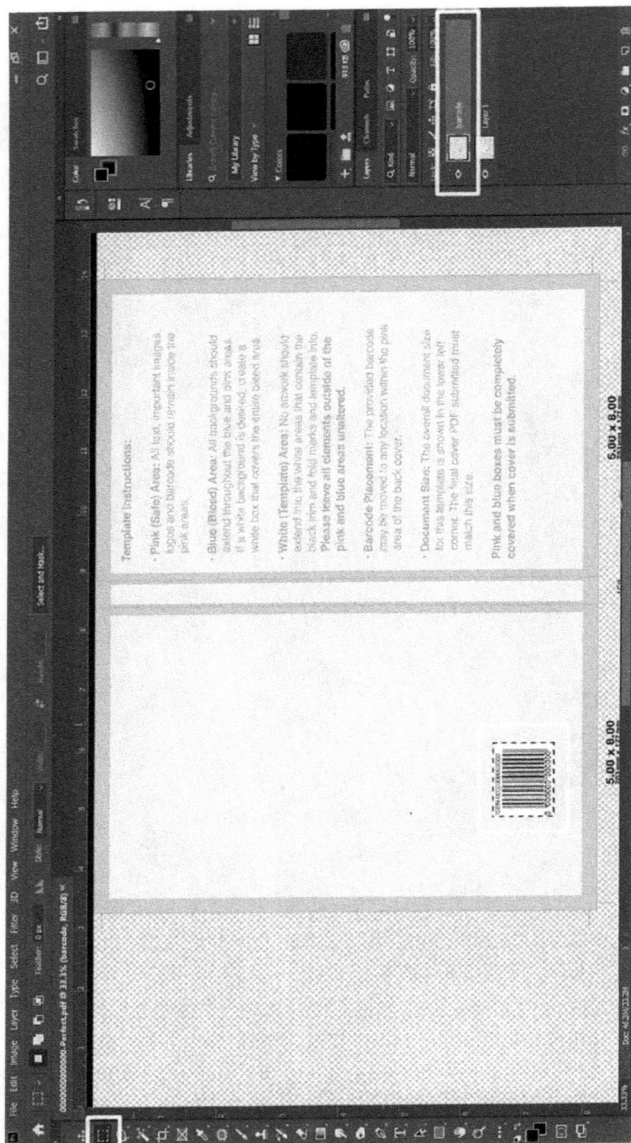

Template Instructions:

- Pink (Safe) Area: All text, important images, logos and barcode should remain inside the pink areas.

- Blue (Bleed) Area: All backgrounds should extend throughout the blue and pink areas. If a white background is desired, create a white box that covers the entire bleed area.

- White (Template) Area: No artwork should extend into the white areas that contain the black trim and fold marks and template info. Please leave all elements outside of the pink and blue areas unaltered.

- Barcode Placement: The provided barcode may be moved to any location within the pink area of the back cover.

- Document Size: The overall document size for this template is shown in the lower left corner. The final cover PDF submitted must match this size.

Pink and blue boxes must be completely covered when cover is submitted.

5.00 x 8.00

5.00 x 8.00

Pic. 7b

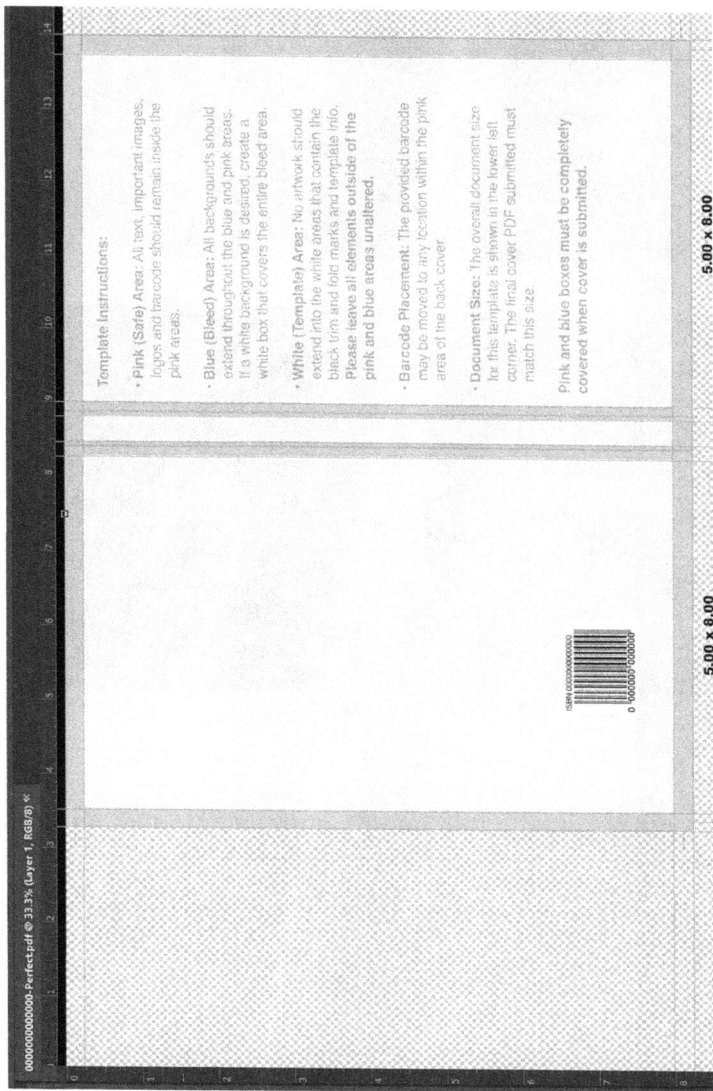

Template Instructions:

· **Pink (Safe) Area:** All text, important images, logos and barcode should remain inside the pink areas.

· **Blue (Bleed) Area:** All backgrounds should extend throughout the blue and pink areas. If a white background is desired, create a white box that covers the entire bleed area.

· **White (Template) Area:** No artwork should extend into the white areas that contain the back trim and fold marks and template info. **Please leave all elements outside of the pink and blue areas unaltered.**

· **Barcode Placement:** The provided barcode may be moved to any location within the pink area of the back cover.

· **Document Size:** The overall document size for this template is shown in the lower left corner. The final cover PDF submitted must match this size.

Pink and blue boxes must be completely covered when cover is submitted.

5.00 x 8.00

5.00 x 8.00

Pic. 7c

Pic. 7d

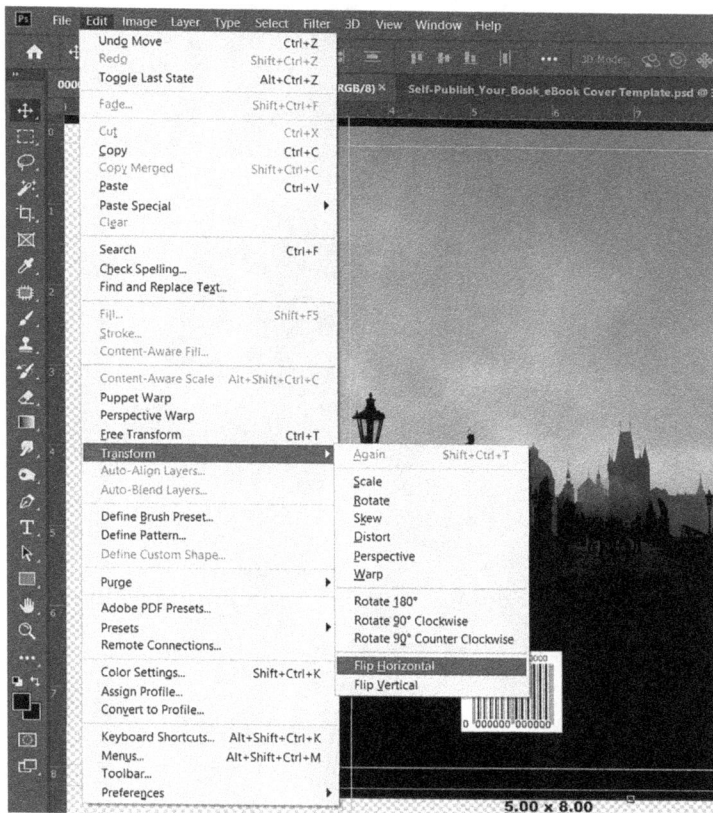

Pic. 7e

Pic. 7f

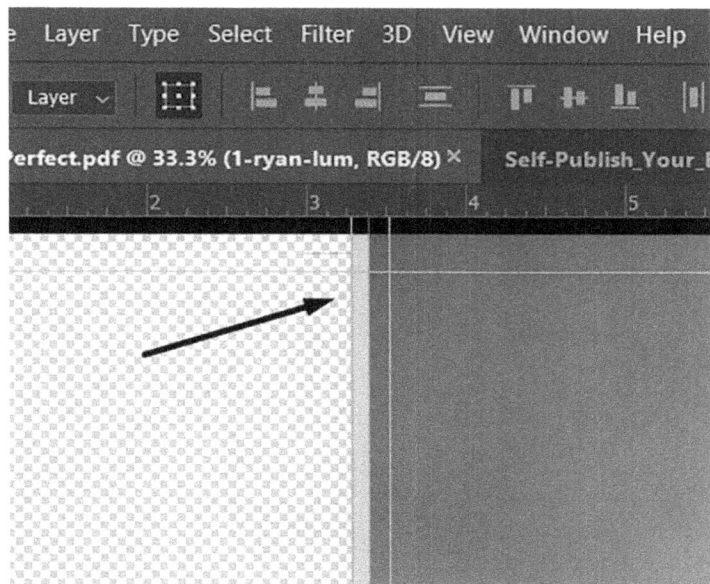

Pic. 7g

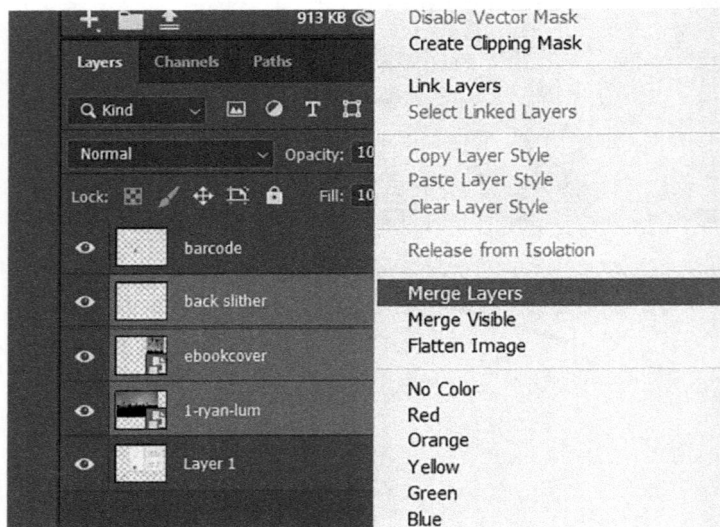

Pic. 7h

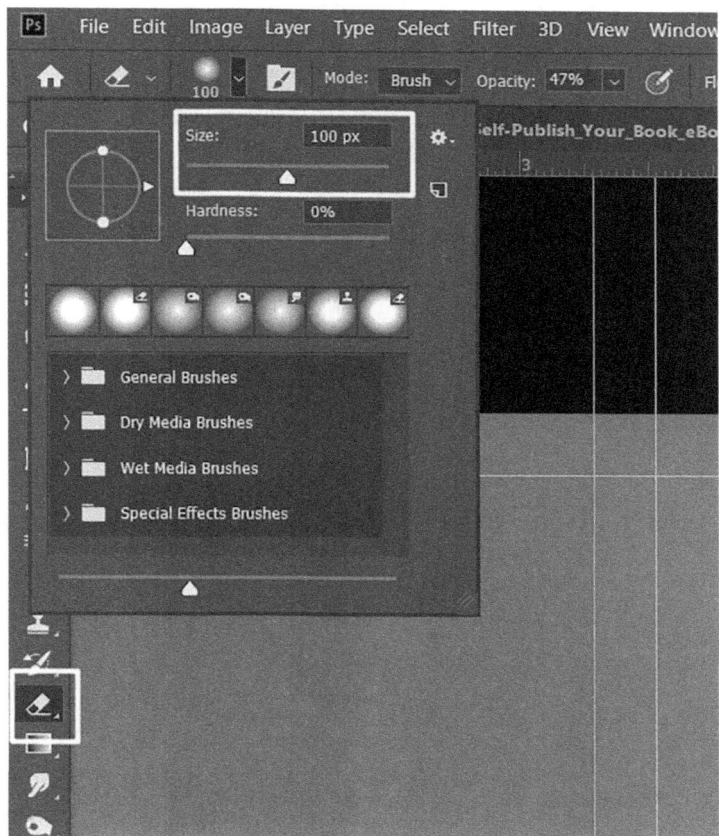

Pic. 7i

AFTER

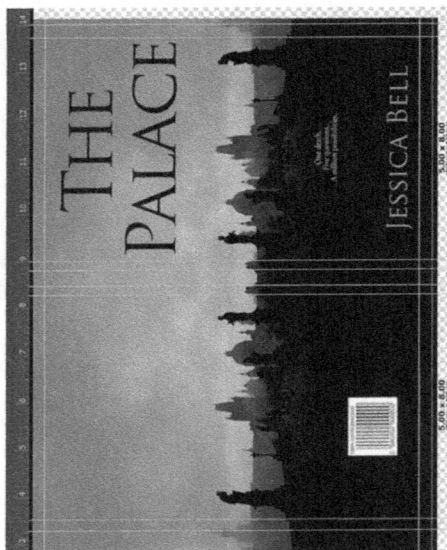

BEFORE

Pic. 7j

Pic. 7k

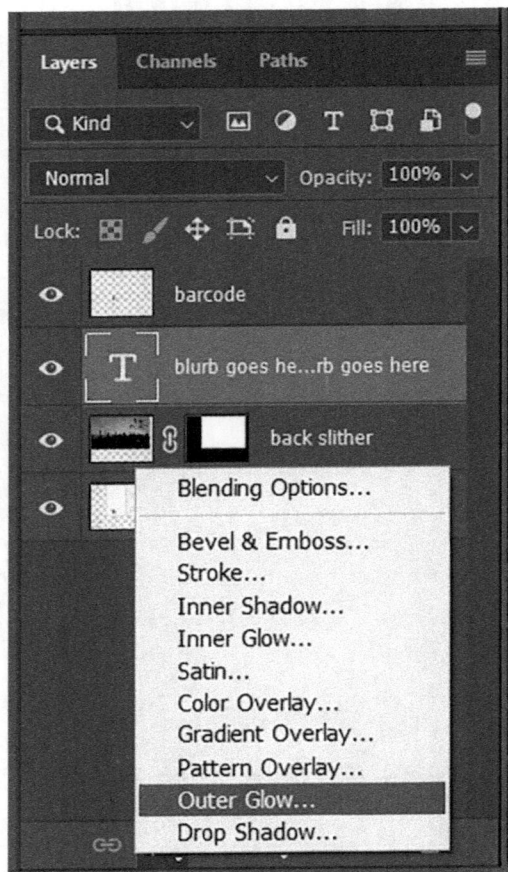

Pic. 71

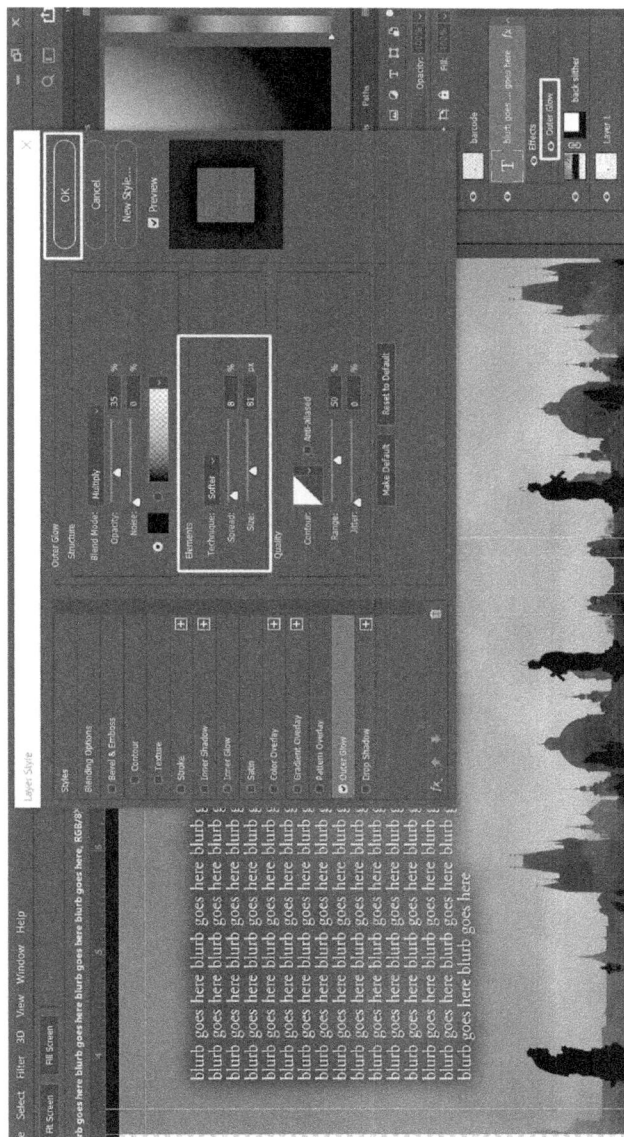

Pic. 7m

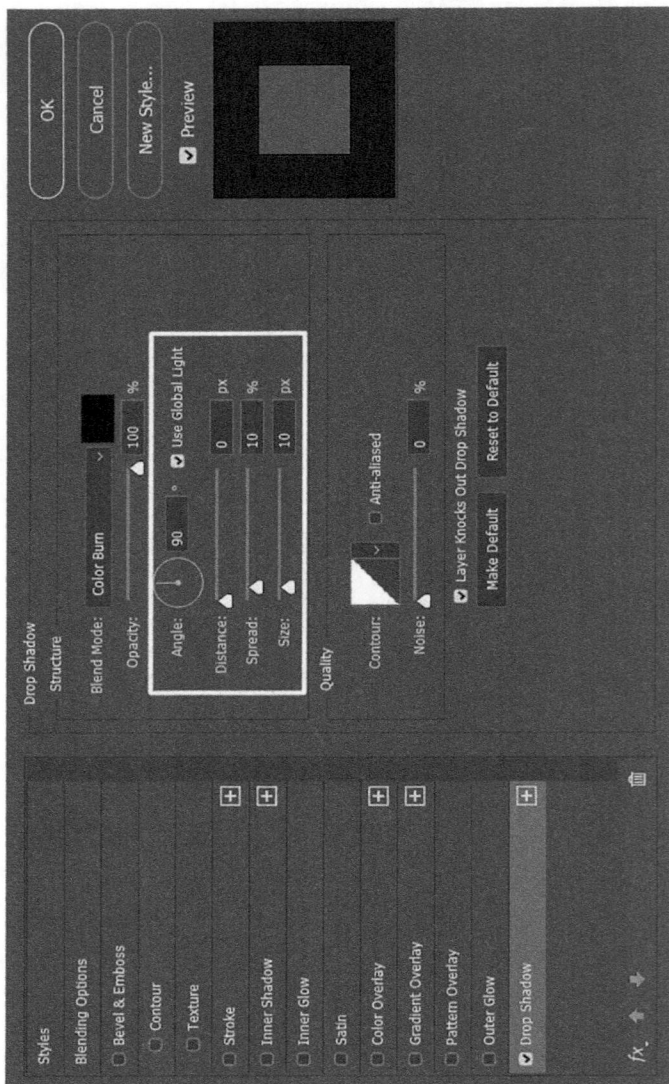

Pic. 7n

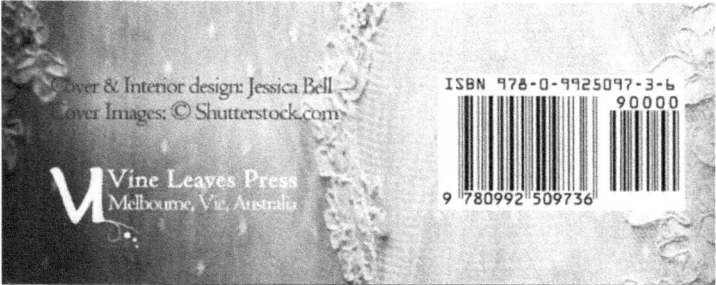

Cover & Interior design: Jessica Bell
Cover Images: © Shutterstock.com

Vine Leaves Press
Melbourne, Vic, Australia

ISBN 978-0-9925097-3-6
90000

9 780992 509736

Pic. 7o

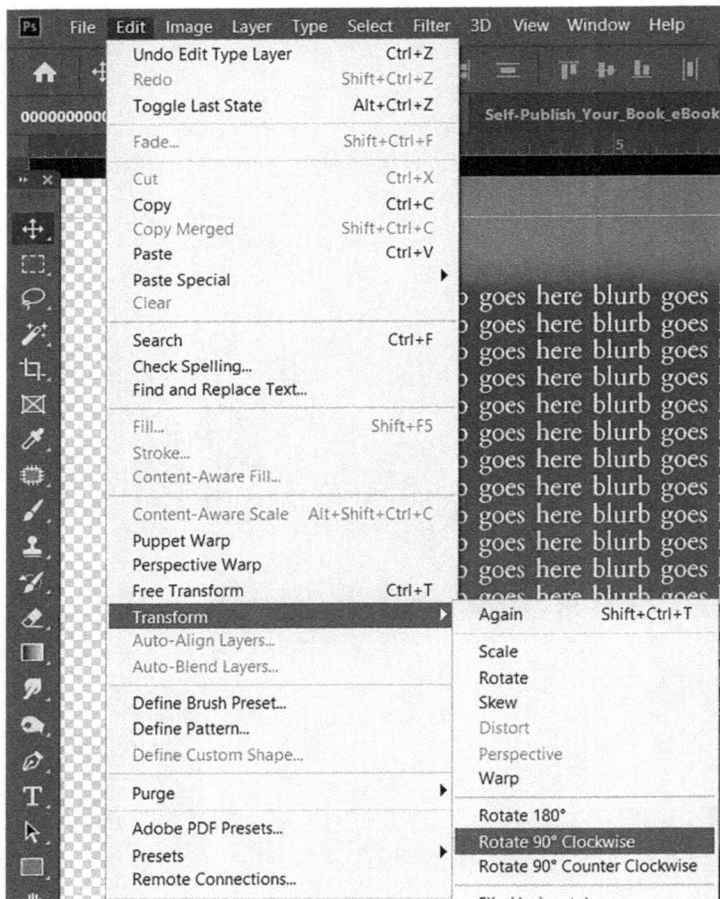

Pic. 7p

THE PALACE

THE PALACE

One death.
Five questions,
A million possibilities.

JESSICA BELL

JESSICA BELL

blurb goes here blurb goes here blurb goes here
blurb goes here blurb goes here blurb goes here
blurb goes here blurb goes here blurb goes here
blurb goes here blurb goes here blurb goes here
blurb goes here blurb goes here blurb goes here
blurb goes here blurb goes here blurb goes here
blurb goes here blurb goes here blurb goes here
blurb goes here blurb goes here blurb goes here
blurb goes here blurb goes here blurb goes here
blurb goes here blurb goes here blurb goes here
blurb goes here blurb goes here blurb goes here
blurb goes here blurb goes here blurb goes here
blurb goes here blurb goes here blurb goes here
blurb goes here blurb goes here blurb goes here
blurb goes here blurb goes here blurb goes here
blurb goes here blurb goes here blurb goes here
blurb goes here blurb goes here

Other information
Other information
Other information

ISBN 000000000000

0 "000000 000000"

Pic. 7q

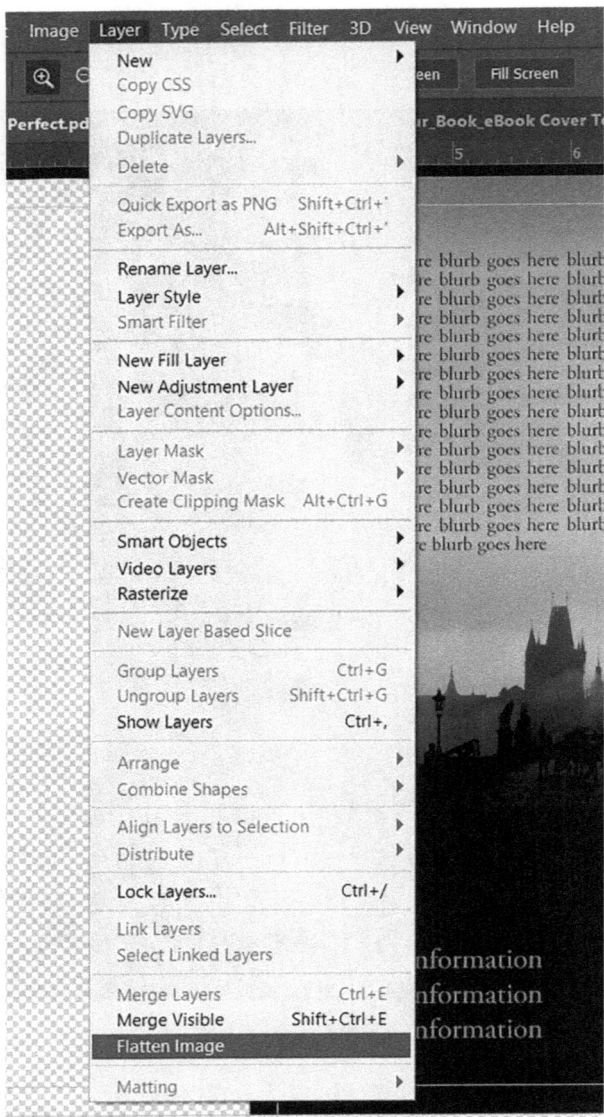

Pic. 7r

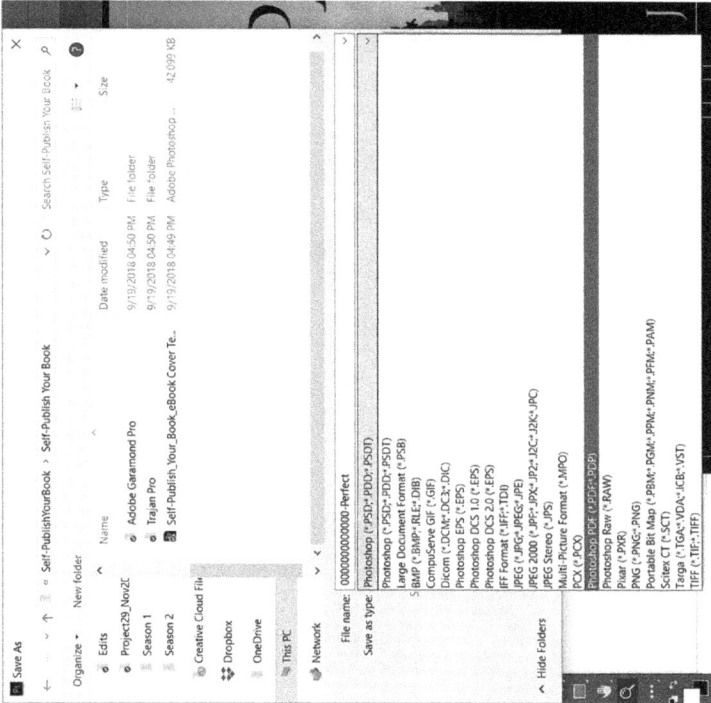

Pic. 7s

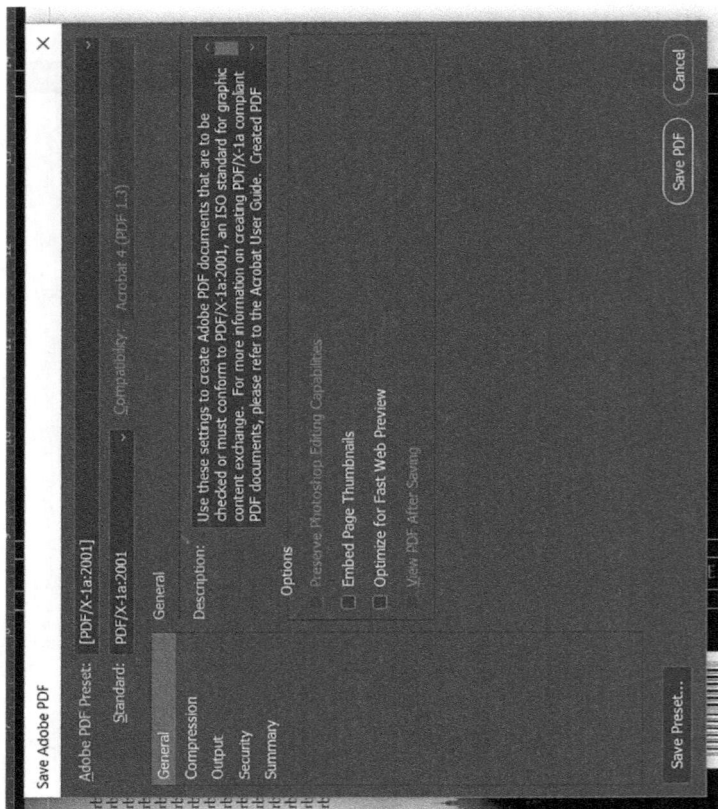

Save Adobe PDF   ✕

Adobe PDF Preset: [PDF/X-1a:2001]

Standard: POF/X-1a:2001   Compatibility: Acrobat 4 (PDF 1.3)

General

General

Compression   Description: Use these settings to create Adobe PDF documents that are to be
Output   checked or must conform to PDF/X-1a:2001, an ISO standard for graphic
Security   content exchange. For more information on creating PDF/X-1a compliant
Summary   PDF documents, please refer to the Acrobat User Guide. Created PDF

Options

□ Preserve Photoshop Editing Capabilities

□ Embed Page Thumbnails

□ Optimize for Fast Web Preview

□ View PDF After Saving

Save Preset...   Save PDF   Cancel

Pic. 7t

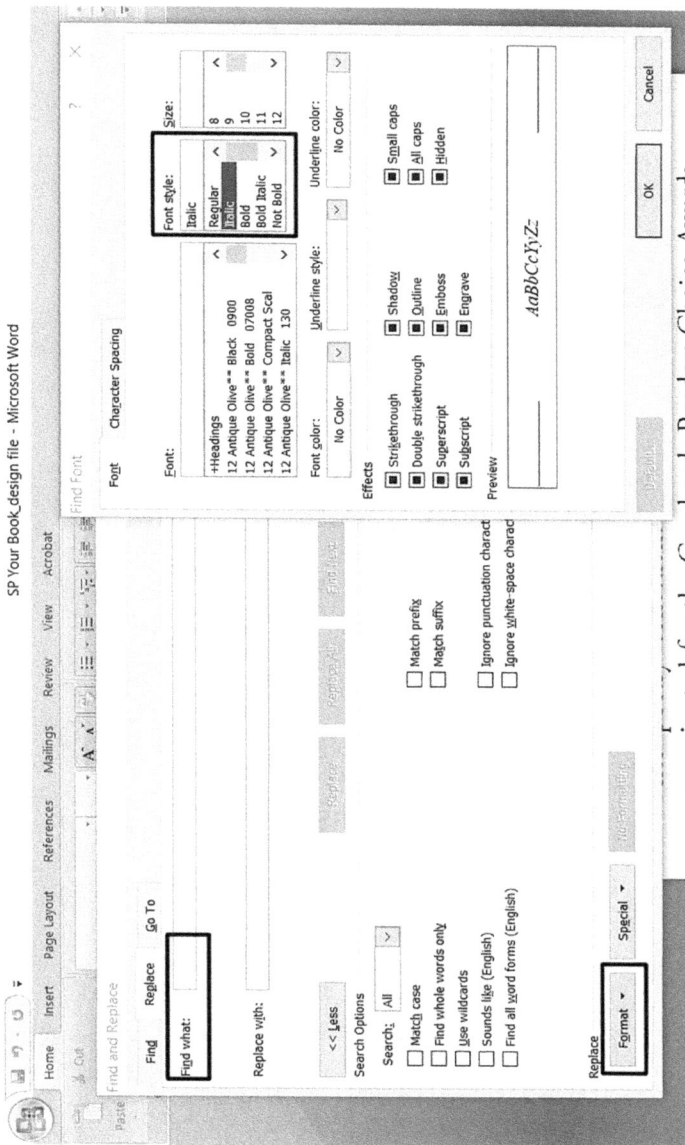

Pic. 8a

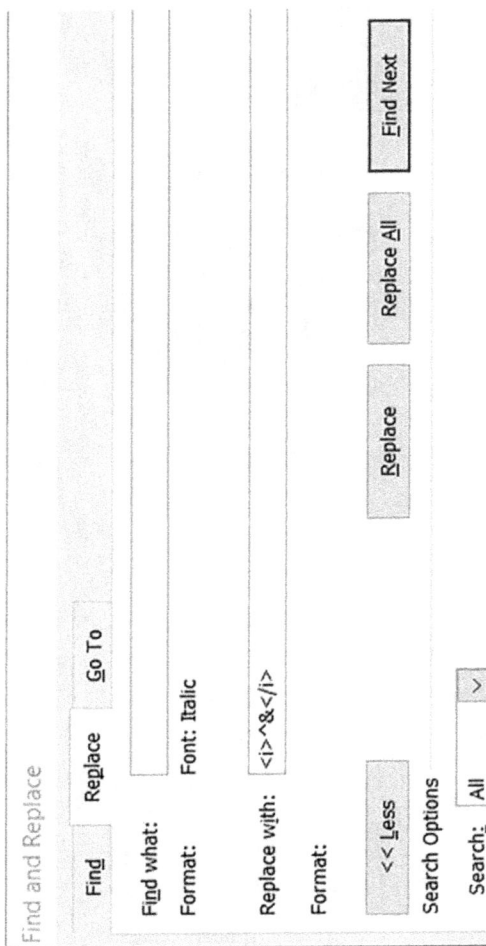

Find and Replace

Find	Replace	Go To

Find what:

Format: Font: Italic

Replace with: <i>^&</i>

Format:

<< Less

Search Options

Search: All   >

Replace   Replace All   Find Next

Pic. 8b

```html
 </style>
 </head>

<body>

<p class="title"><span class="centered">YOUR TITLE</span></p>
<p class="authorname"><span class="centered">YOUR NAME</span></

<p class="dedication"><span class="centered"><i>Dedication</i>

<p class="chap"><span class="centered">Chapter 1</span></p>
<p class="chaptitle"><span class="centered">Your Chapter Title
<p class="first">The first paragraph of your chapter goes here
<p>The rest of your chapter goes here.</p>

<p class="chap"><span class="centered">Chapter 2</span></p>
<p class="chaptitle"><span class="centered">Your Chapter Title
<p class="first">The first paragraph of your chapter goes here
<p>The rest of your chapter goes here.</p>
```

Pic. 8c

File Edit Search View Encoding Language Settings Tools Macro Run Plugins

eBook_Interior_Template.html

```html
127    <p class="title"><span class="centered">YOUR TITLE</span></p>
128    <p class="authorname"><span class="centered">YOUR NAME</span></p>
129
130    <p class="dedication"><span class="centered"><i>Dedication</i></span>
131
132    <p class="chap"><span class="centered">Chapter 1</span></p>
133    <p class="chaptitle"><span class="centered">Your Chapter Title. Remov
134    <p class="first">The first paragraph of your chapter goes here.</p>
135    <p>The rest of your chapter goes here.</p>
136
137    <p class="chap"><span class="centered">Chapter 2</span></p>
138    <p class="chaptitle"><span class="centered">Your Chapter Title. Remov
139    <p class="first">The first paragraph of your chapter goes here.</p>
140    <p>The rest of your chapter goes here.</p>
141
142    <p class="chap"><span class="centered">Chapter 3</span></p>
143    <p class="chaptitle"><span class="centered">Your Chapter Title. Remov
144    <p class="first">The first paragraph of your chapter goes here.</p>
145    <p>The rest of your chapter goes here.</p>
```

Pic. 8d

```html
<p class="chap"><span class="centered">Chapter 1</span></p>
<p class="chaptitle"><span class="centered">Your Chapter Title. Remove this whole line if you don't have one. If you'd like to use the title instead of "Chapter 1", insert it in the line above.</span></p>
<p class="first">The first paragraph of your chapter goes here.</p>
<p>The rest of your chapter goes here.</p>

<p class="chap"><span class="centered">Chapter 2</span></p>
<p class="chaptitle"><span class="centered">Your Chapter Title. Remove this whole line if you don't have one. If you'd like to use the title instead of "Chapter 1", insert it in the line above.</span></p>
<p class="first">The first paragraph of your chapter goes here.</p>
<p>The rest of your chapter goes here.</p>

<p class="chap"><span class="centered">Chapter 3</span></p>
<p class="chaptitle"><span class="centered">Your Chapter Title. Remove this whole line if you don't have one. If you'd like to use the title instead of "Chapter 1", insert it in the line above.</span></p>
<p class="first">The first paragraph of your chapter goes here.</p>
<p>The rest of your chapter goes here.</p>

<p class="chap"><span class="centered">Chapter 4</span></p>
<p class="chaptitle"><span class="centered">Your Chapter Title. Remove this whole line if you don't have one. If you'd like to use the title instead of "Chapter 1", insert it in the line above.</span></p>
<p class="first">The first paragraph of your chapter goes here.</p>
<p>The rest of your chapter goes here.</p>

<p class="chap"><span class="centered">Chapter 5</span></p>
<p class="chaptitle"><span class="centered">Your Chapter Title. Remove this whole line if you don't have one. If you'd like to use the title instead of "Chapter 1", insert it in the line above.</span></p>
<p class="first">The first paragraph of your chapter goes here.</p>
<p>The rest of your chapter goes here.</p>
```

Pic. 8e

Find and Replace

Find	Replace	Go To

Find what: ^(.+)$

Replace with: <p>^&</p>

| << Less | | Replace | Replace All | Find Next |

Search Options

Pic. 8f

```
File Edit Search View Encoding Language Settings Tools Macro Run Plugins Window ?

eBook_Basic_Template.html

<p class="title"><span class="centered">YOUR TITLE</span></p>
<p class="authorname"><span class="centered">YOUR NAME</span></p>

<p class="dedication"><span class="centered"><i>Dedication</i></span></p>

<p class="chap"><span class="centered">Chapter 1</span></p>
<p class="chaptitle"><span class="centered">Your Chapter Title. Remove this whole line if you don't have one. If you'd like to use the title instead of "Chapter 1", insert it in the line above.</span></p>
<p class="first">The first paragraph of your chapter goes here.</p>
<p>The rest of your chapter goes here.</p>

<p class="chap"><span class="centered">Chapter 2</span></p>
<p class="chaptitle"><span class="centered">Your Chapter Title. Remove this whole line if you don't have one. If you'd like to use the title instead of "Chapter 1", insert it in the line above.</span></p>
<p class="first">The first paragraph of your chapter goes here.</p>
<p>The rest of your chapter goes here.</p>

<p class="chap"><span class="centered">Chapter 3</span></p>
<p class="chaptitle"><span class="centered">Your Chapter Title. Remove this whole line if you don't have one. If you'd like to use the title instead of "Chapter 1", insert it in the line above.</span></p>
<p class="first">The first paragraph of your chapter goes here.</p>
<p>The rest of your chapter goes here.</p>

<p class="chap"><span class="centered">Chapter 4</span></p>
<p class="chaptitle"><span class="centered">Your Chapter Title. Remove this whole line if you don't have one. If you'd like to use the title instead of "Chapter 1", insert it in the line above.</span></p>
<p class="first">The first paragraph of your chapter goes here.</p>
<p>The rest of your chapter goes here.</p>

<p class="chap"><span class="centered">Chapter 5</span></p>
<p class="chaptitle"><span class="centered">Your Chapter Title. Remove this whole line if you don't have one. If you'd like to use the title instead of "Chapter 1", insert it in the line above.</span></p>
<p class="first">The first paragraph of your chapter goes here.</p>
<p>The rest of your chapter goes here.</p>

<p class="chap"><span class="centered">Chapter 6</span></p>
<p class="chaptitle"><span class="centered">Your Chapter Title. Remove this whole line if you don't have one. If you'd like to use the title instead of "Chapter 1", insert it in the line above.</span></p>
<p class="first">The first paragraph of your chapter goes here.</p>
<p>The rest of your chapter goes here.</p>
```

Pic. 8g

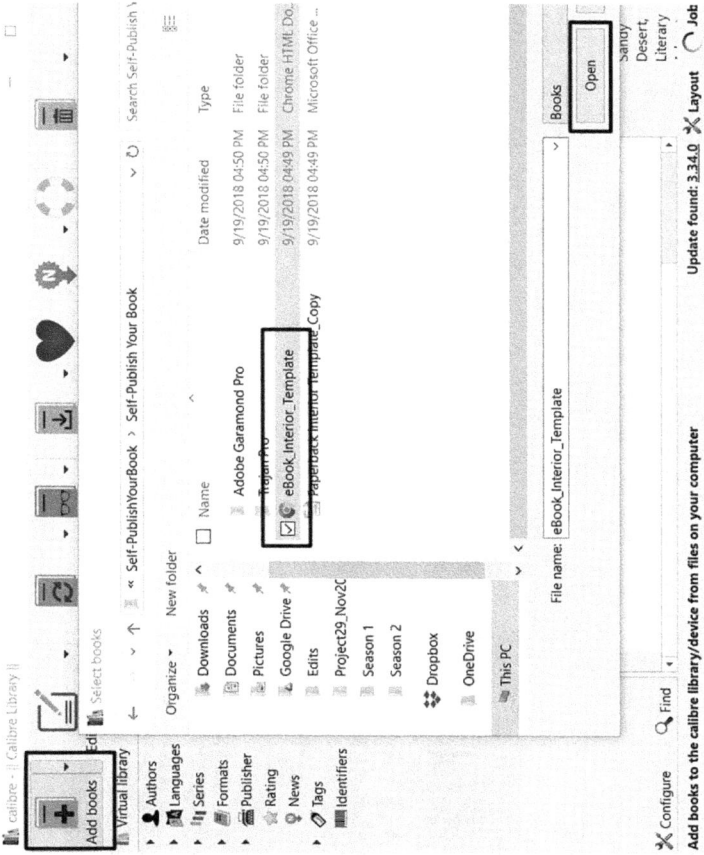

Pic. 9a

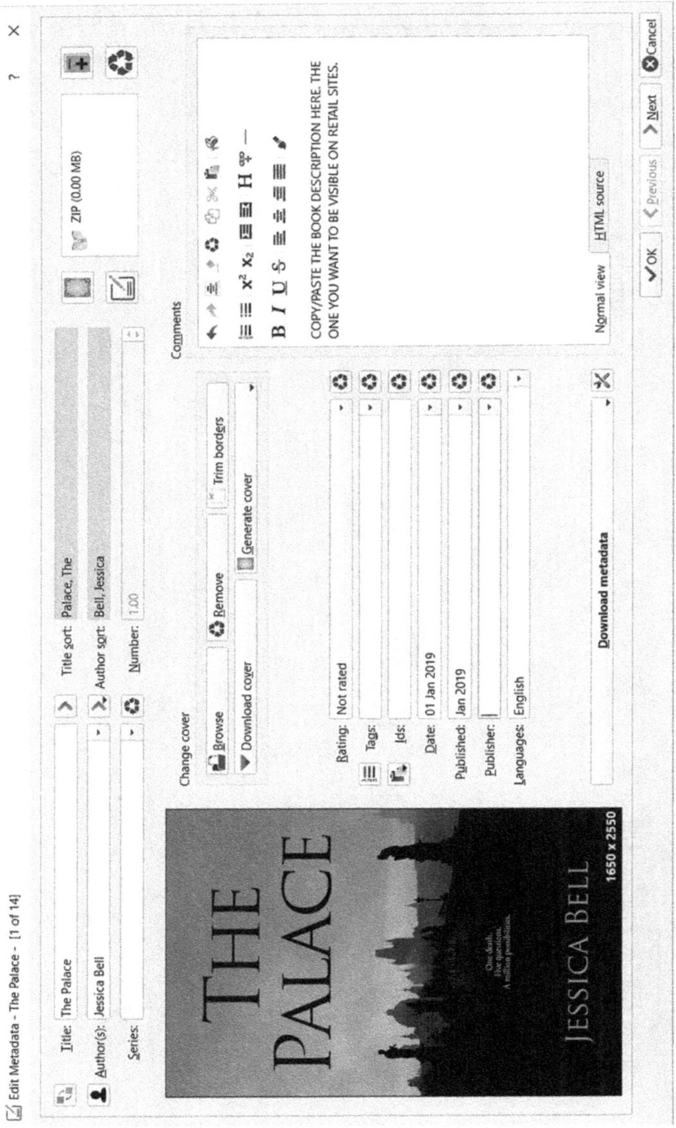
Edit Metadata - The Palace - [1 of 14]
Title: The Palace
Title sort: Palace, The
Author(s): Jessica Bell
Author sort: Bell, Jessica
Series:
Number: 1.00
ZIP (0.00 MB)
Change cover
Browse
Remove
Trim borders
Download cover
Generate cover
THE PALACE
JESSICA BELL
1650 x 2550
Rating: Not rated
Tags:
Ids:
Date: 01 Jan 2019
Published: Jan 2019
Publisher:
Languages: English
Download metadata
Comments
COPY/PASTE THE BOOK DESCRIPTION HERE. THE ONE YOU WANT TO BE VISIBLE ON RETAIL SITES.
Normal view
HTML source
OK
Previous
Next
Cancel

Pic. 9b

Pic. 9c

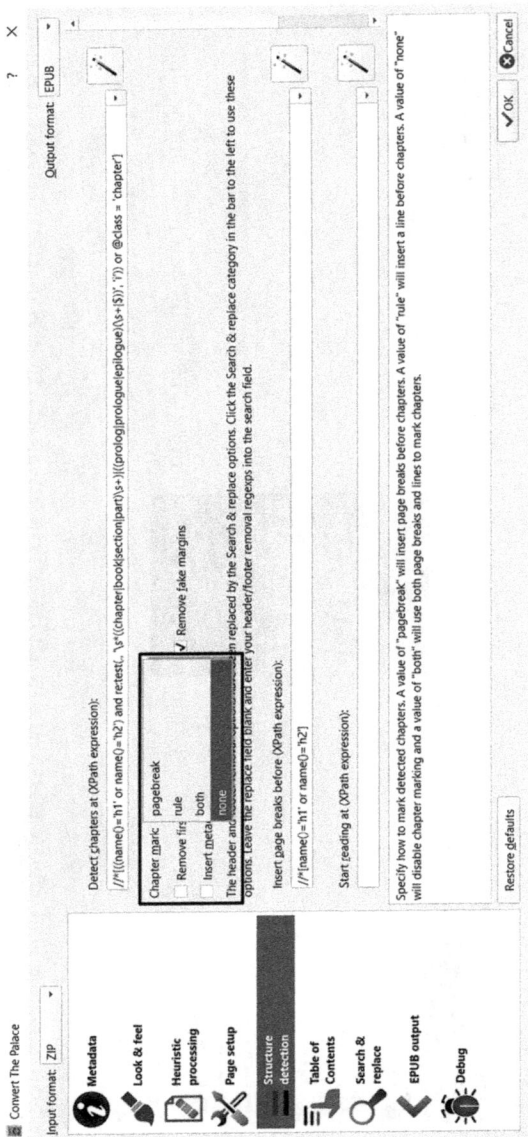

Convert The Palace

Input format: ZIP   Output format: EPUB

- Metadata
- Look & feel
- Heuristic processing
- Page setup
- **Structure detection**
- Table of Contents
- Search & replace
- EPUB output
- Debug

Detect chapters at (XPath expression):

`//*[((name()='h1' or name()='h2') and re:test(., '\s*((chapter|book|section|part)|\s+)?((prologue|prologue|epilogue)(\s+|$))', 'i')) or @class = 'chapter']`

√ Remove fake margins

Chapter mark: pagebreak

- Remove firs: rule
- Insert meta: both
-   none

The header and .... replaced by the Search & replace options. Click the Search & replace category in the bar to the left to use these options. Leave the replace field blank and enter your header/footer removal regexps into the search field.

Insert page breaks before (XPath expression):

`//*[name()='h1' or name()='h2']`

Start reading at (XPath expression):

`//*[name()='h1' or name()='h2']`

Specify how to mark detected chapters. A value of "pagebreak" will insert page breaks before chapters. A value of "rule" will insert a line before chapters. A value of "none" will disable chapter marking and a value of "both" will use both page breaks and lines to mark chapters.

Restore defaults   ✔ OK   ✖ Cancel

Pic. 9d

Convert The Palace

Input format: ZIP ▼

Metadata

Look & feel

Heuristic processing

Page setup

Structure detection

Table of Contents

Search & replace

EPUB output

Debug

Force use of auto-generated Table of Contents

☐ Do not add detected chapters to the Table of Contents

☐ Allow duplicate links when creating the Table of Contents

Number of links to add to Table of Contents: 50

Chapter threshold: 6

TOC filter:

Level 1 TOC (XPath expression):

//h:p[re:test(@class, "chap", "i")]

Level 2 TOC (XPath expression):

Level 3 TOC (XPath expression):

✓ Manually fine-tune the ToC after conversion is completed

XPath expression that specifies all tags that should be added to
Tutorial in the calibre User Manual for examples.

Restore defaults

Pic. 9e

Pic. 9f

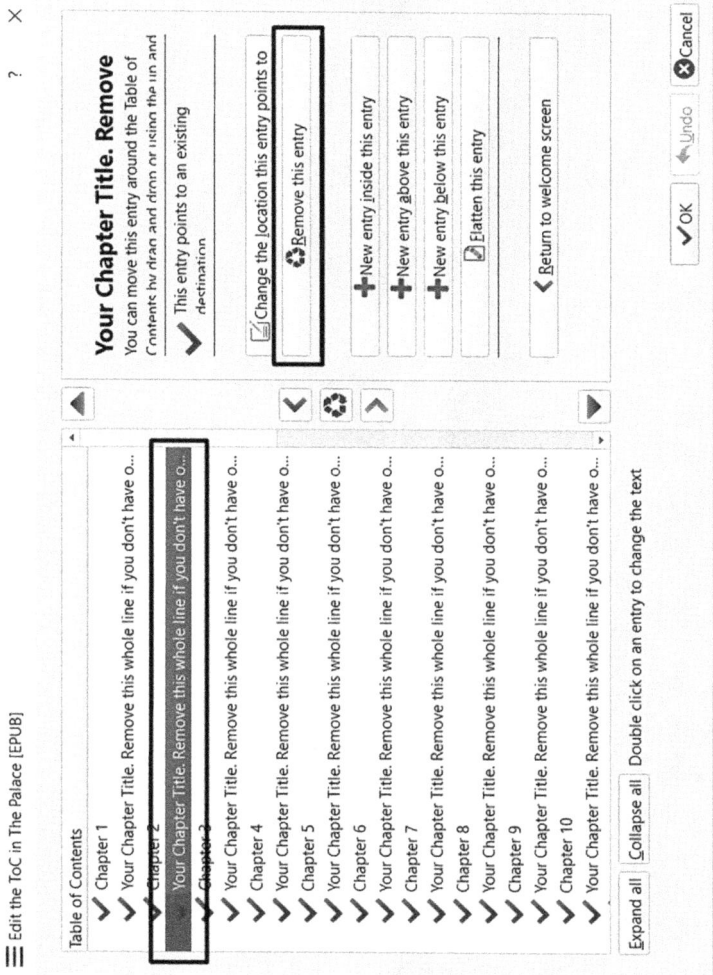

Edit the ToC in The Palace [EPUB]

Table of Contents

- Chapter 1
  - Your Chapter Title. Remove this whole line if you don't have o...
- Chapter 2
  - Your Chapter Title. Remove this whole line if you don't have o...
- Chapter 3
  - Your Chapter Title. Remove this whole line if you don't have o...
- Chapter 4
  - Your Chapter Title. Remove this whole line if you don't have o...
- Chapter 5
  - Your Chapter Title. Remove this whole line if you don't have o...
- Chapter 6
  - Your Chapter Title. Remove this whole line if you don't have o...
- Chapter 7
  - Your Chapter Title. Remove this whole line if you don't have o...
- Chapter 8
  - Your Chapter Title. Remove this whole line if you don't have o...
- Chapter 9
  - Your Chapter Title. Remove this whole line if you don't have o...
- Chapter 10
  - Your Chapter Title. Remove this whole line if you don't have o...

Expand all | Collapse all | Double click on an entry to change the text

Your Chapter Title. Remove

You can move this entry around the Table of Contents by drag and drop or using the up and

- This entry points to an existing destination

- Change the location this entry points to
- Remove this entry
- New entry inside this entry
- New entry above this entry
- New entry below this entry
- Flatten this entry
- Return to welcome screen

OK | Undo | Cancel

Pic. 9g

Name	Date modified	Type	Size
Palace, The - Jessica Bell	12/2/2018 04:21 PM	EPUB Document	462 KB
Palace, The - Jessica Bell	12/2/2018 04:21 PM	JPG File	444 KB
Palace, The - Jessica Bell	12/2/2018 04:21 PM	OPF Document	2 KB
Palace, The - Jessica Bell	12/2/2018 04:21 PM	Compressed (zipp...	3 KB

Pic. 9h